DATE DUE

MAR 1 7 2009

CHILD-CENTRED EDUCATION

Child-Centred Education

REVIVING THE CREATIVE TRADITION

Christine Doddington and Mary Hilton

SAGE Publications
Los Angeles • London • New Delhi • Singapore

SAGE Publications Ltd
1 Oliver's Yard
55 City Road
London EC1Y 1SP

SAGE Publications Inc.
2455 Teller Road
Thousand Oaks, California 91320

SAGE Publications India Pvt Ltd
B 1/I 1 Mohan Cooperative Industrial Area
Mathura Road
New Delhi 110 044

SAGE Publications Asia-Pacific Pte Ltd
33 Pekin Street #02-01
Far East Square
Singapore 048763

Library of Congress Control Number: 2007925065

British Library Cataloguing in Publication data

A catalogue record for this book is available from the British Library

ISBN 978-1-4129-4587-5
ISBN 978-1-4129-4588-2 (pbk)
Typeset by Dorwyn, Wells, Somerset
Printed in Great Britain by Athenaeum Press, Gateshead, Tyne & Wear
Printed on paper from sustainable resources

To all those teachers
who hold to values and practices that, despite opposition,
continue to enrich the child-centred tradition

contents

preface

This book sets out to explore the history and philosophy of child-centredness in primary education in order to revive its creative strengths in a time of increasing anxiety about the nation's children. As the testing and grading of children continues to intensify, the primary curriculum is increasingly becoming narrower and more arid. The arts, play and experimentation that we feel should be part of every child's day, and which we will argue are essential to intellectual and spiritual growth, are now bracketed off into small segments of curriculum time. Particularly in Britain, but also elsewhere, teachers are continuously exhorted to teach to instrumental and narrow objectives. Meanwhile many children are increasingly bored and disaffected. Primary disciplinary exclusions in Britain have risen dramatically, while truancy, once a small concern around a tiny number of children, has now become a national scandal in numbers and extent. Nor have standards risen. New research shows that the present British government have exaggerated the effects of their 'standards agenda'. While some children and their teachers have become successfully tuned to doing tests, many of the remainder, starved of interest and pleasure in learning, languish in an atmosphere of anxiety and disaffection.

In fact new initiatives show that many politicians, government agencies, academics and parents are still concerned about our primary schools. This is not simply a 'left-wing' reaction to the tightening of authority, hierarchy and control over the curriculum. Across the political spectrum Britain's lively enterprise culture is beginning to be seen as dependent on creativity that must be encouraged and fostered in schools. A search is on for the roots of creative thought, for 'thinking skills' and for the culture of enterprise, particularly in design and technology. Indeed, within a global culture that embraces the new technologies of the information age it has become essential to produce young citizens that produce, and consume, in creative and ever-changing ways. Fast capitalism demands invention and flexibility towards lifestyle that must be engendered and fostered in the young. However, what is at stake here is not simply another argument over curriculum content but the inner lives and development of children themselves. To be simply considered as units in future economic schemas puts children and their precious time of childhood, when they develop socially, emotionally, morally and intellectually, into a narrow, instrumental and damaging educational process that ignores the vital ways children learn how to be, how to learn and how to create. Alienation and anomie, truancy and crime, may be the price we have to pay if we continue to bully and to constrain children within restrictive educational practices.

What is crucial here is that Britain, among other nations, already has deep roots in an alternative and progressive educational culture. Far from being a pernicious socialist idea thought up in the 1960s and then spread like a contagious disease into primary schools as it is often represented, we argue that child-centred education lies at the heart of Britain's success in the industrial age and has continuously supported a liberal outward-looking culture of optimism and progress. We believe that it is time to return to the rich heritage of this ideology of childhood learning. In this book we analyse the fundamental values embedded in child-centred education and trace its growth from the English Enlightenment through the nineteenth and twentieth centuries. We examine how the ideas of childhood agency, personhood and active intellectual development grew in lively opposition to authoritarian and ineffectual educational practices. We examine this indigenous educational philosophy, which was eventually shaped and developed by German, British, European and American thinkers and teachers, and explore some of its repeated structuring ideas that open creative possibilities for the education of children. We look at the ways that we might build on this rich legacy and begin, through bringing philosophical ideas to bear, to construct a twenty-first-century version of child-centred education. In the final chapter we point to the ways that schools and practice would need to be reformed to revive this creative tradition.

introduction

This book offers a reappraisal of child-centred education through describing its unique history within Britain since the Enlightenment and examining its basic principles. We do not begin with the many practices that might be considered child centred. Instead, we set out to unravel the complex nature of child-centred education by considering its historical and philosophical roots, and by contrasting these with the alternative views it has traditionally contested – in the past and still in current educational thought. We ask, what is it to be a child? What should the lived experience of school offer the young learner and the adult teacher? And how does our view of the critical relationship between teacher and child derive from our most deeply held values? To this purpose we consider the historical forces, beliefs and arguments that have shaped our ideas of childhood education, relating these questions to our systems of underlying values and beliefs. In this way we can begin to see the kinds of ideas and values that those who hold to child-centredness, here and across the world, deem to be crucial in education, and to find similarities and common aims in schools and classrooms, even when specific practices seem to vary. But before we focus on children and education we should consider the role that values play in our lives more generally.

THE INEVITABILITY OF VALUES

So how do values actually work to characterize people or, as in our specific case, the nature of a complex human enterprise like education? Values that underpin our ways of living are basically embedded in, and grow from, our held beliefs. Often these beliefs are moral, concerning how we should behave towards others in this world, so if we believe in being honest and value honesty in others this means that we try to avoid deceiving others and frown on deceit in others. We call on this value when we make decisions and judgements about what to do or how we should proceed. However, life's dilemmas are never straightforward. All too often we are faced with several ideas that we hold dear and sometimes they can be inconsistent or in conflict with one another – we want to be honest, but sometimes if we say what we think we may hurt someone's feelings. Which is more important, to speak the truth or prevent someone from feeling hurt? The point here is that we do not and cannot use our values as if they are rules. We have to use our judgement flexibly in each situation where honesty or caring for someone's feelings becomes an issue. We have to work out where the emphasis should be in *this* particular case and judge what the priority is *here* and at this time.

In educational decision-making and judgements values work in a similar way. In a professional educational context, the beliefs and values that guide practice form the principles by which sensitive judgements and decisions are made, and decisions or judgements are rarely made on the basis of a single value. What we value in education is likely to be complicated because it will depend on our priorities and what we consider 'the good' to be for people, for lives and for society. Therefore values are likely to pervade any discussion about education and what its practice should be like. Individuals will expose their value positions in any rich or sustained discussion about 'what we should do' or 'what needs to happen' even if no one asks them to make these explicit. However, one important distinction we should make between personal values and educational values is that we see teachers as professionals and governors as doing a public duty, so that their values that influence practice should not be seen as simply idiosyncratic personal ones, but should be publicly explicit, justified and agreed. Individual teachers often need to exercise judgement in terms of priorities in ways that are sensitive to the particularities of a situation, but discussion and decisions about what we think collectively *as a school* is crucial to determining the ways our children work, what they study or the way we all relate to one another, giving principles and values by which the school can stand. They provide a basis which hopefully influences all those necessarily pragmatic, individual, day-to-day decisions and judgements that have to be made in schools. However, in the field of education it needs to be acknowledged that it is sometimes difficult to clarify values that are implicit and embedded in personal perspectives and the way we think. One strategy that helps us to highlight and examine values is to contrast them with beliefs that contradict what we think and feel (rejecting deceit, helps to clarify what honesty is for us, for example). For this reason, in the chapters that look at child-centred values in education we contrast them with sets of often deeply felt, alternative value systems.

Clearly, ongoing discussion about values in schools is not just desirable but necessary. However, genuine discussion also implies that values can evolve and change. This is an important view to have but it also needs a word of caution, for values cannot be changed or swapped in a random, piecemeal way in the same way as we might change one coloured sweater for another. Values come into play in both our lives and professionally in schools, in a connection with other values. They interlink to form coherent frameworks that give us particular standpoints towards life and similarly towards education. As we see in Chapter 2 of this book, two strong-minded dedicated teachers, both of whom worked in primary education for many years, held to deeply opposing values. Their very different ideologies of childhood shaped their whole professional lives. Because value-laden frameworks that are set out clearly and tested through discussion can be both strong and coherent they are able to offer not just a basis for clear and decisive action, but can also generate the *will* to act, by inspiring conviction in those that feel they own and hold them dear. We believe that conviction and commitment to a set of values is thus a vital part of teaching well.

THE CURRENT STATE OF DISCUSSION ABOUT VALUES

In Britain and in many parts of the world we are currently in an educational context where prescription is on the ascendant and teachers are required to 'implement' and 'deliver' prescribed skills and knowledge, and have to be seen to do so. Added to this is the assumption that education can be prescribed without even thinking about values or the aims that these values generate. Indeed, as late as 1988 in Britain when a National Curriculum was first published, those policy-makers and civil servants who constructed the curriculum did not even think they needed to articulate their overall purposes at all.

It was only after much criticism that a version of the values, aims and purposes that might be seen to underpin the curriculum statements was finally published in the 1999 version. In this context of a highly prescribed curriculum a great deal of judgement and decision-making is removed from the classroom teacher and when this happens, his or her values tend to become ignored and sink from view or consideration. This book claims that restricting the work of beliefs and values in teachers' thinking comes at a high cost. With over-prescription and extensive monitoring, teaching can become a set of depersonalized strategies so that individual initiative and creative thought become too risky. Heavy bureaucratic requirements can leave teachers feeling they can make and own few of their decisions. It is conceivable that this restriction in the capacity to exercise judgement could contribute to teachers feeling demoralized, without control and, even, disaffected. Becoming estranged from the perceived needs of children in this way, teachers lose the very instinctual joy at working with, and sympathy for, young learners that brought them into the profession in the first place.

Even when values are not stated explicitly, any broadly coherent system of education is nevertheless set within a complex web of values. In democratic societies there is usually rightful pressure to expose or explicitly set out these values. This is because a democracy requires that important aspects of any public enterprise, especially one that quite literally affects current and future lives, should be open for debate. The values and assumptions which underpin the current state of education across the globe are both complex and contested. Features such as measurement and 'performativity' for both children and schools have become paramount in many nations. Nevertheless these have, at various stages and from many quarters, been strongly critiqued. Should we place a high value only on educational performance that can be measured? Some argue that the urge or demand to measure performance has succeeded in significantly shifting and re-forming how education is promoted and practised. In a democracy then, there is the need to ask hard questions to see if these and other current values *are* the most important for our young citizens.

So considering alternative, and even contrasting, values may open the box of implicit assumptions in educational policy and practice, provide food for thought and, even, generate the impetus to see education differently. This is why this book is devoted to looking quite specifically at lessons that can be learned from history and at some of the central values that have always, it will be argued, underpinned a sense of child-centredness. In this way it may be possible to see if a rigorous and coherent alternative to the prevalent instrumental view of education is worth pursuing. Here we argue that some of the values first raised and discussed in the European Enlightenment, and then honed in different, often alternative, nineteenth- and twentieth-century school systems across the world, not only have deep roots in British culture, but are of lasting importance to a liberal democracy in the modern world. Here some of the most significant values centre on the character and nature of the child. The old Puritan assumption that all children, from the moment of birth, are in a state of fallen grace from which they have to be saved, coloured much educational thinking before the Enlightenment. This belief was revived again within the evangelical movement in the early nineteenth century. Only once this belief is challenged and turned on its head can utterly different views of the child emerge, views that stress his or her manifest subjectivity, playfulness and creativity. We argue that these more child-centred values centring on the subjectivity of the learning child emerged in Britain and Europe during the age of the Enlightenment, and became of enduring importance to a liberal view of the family, the school and the political state.

Rousseau   Many historians have argued that a child-centred vision developed alongside and in opposition to the authoritarian structure of the nineteenth-century school system. Sometimes called 'a footnote to Rousseau', history has it that the idea of a 'Romantic child' developed in the late eighteenth century and remained a disturbing and somewhat futile minority movement when it came to educating vast numbers of the industrial poor (Darling, 1994). Yet child-centredness and its associated values have long-standing and deep roots in British, European and American cultures, and the idea of childhood as a separate state of existence has energized debates on education for many centuries. Despite historiographical theories that childhood was 'invented' in the eighteenth century, the historian Linda Pollock demonstrates through examining unpublished family letters and diaries that children have always been loved and their playfulness enjoyed and valued by caring adults around them (Pollock, 1983). From the Renaissance onwards writers such as Erasmus, Bacon and Comenius pointed out that the interest and pleasure of the young learner was essential to his or her true education. Nevertheless, it is clear that the widespread intellectual take-up of the basic child-centred idea – that the morals and intellect of the developing child are a product of his or her environment, rather than of innate ideas and sinfulness – took place in Britain and Europe in the eighteenth century, in the age of the Enlightenment. One of the key figures in this massive change in values was John Locke.

'I CONSIDER THEM AS CHILDREN, WHO MUST BE TENDERLY USED'

Locke By the end of the seventeenth century Puritan culture, which had dominated the rearing of children in England, was in retreat. Within its system of beliefs an adult's duty was clear. Without extensive intervention to 'break' their wills, children would remain in a state of damnation. Biblical sources upheld this view: 'Thou shalt beat him with a rod, and shalt deliver his soul from hell' (Proverbs 23:14). However, by the end of that century a worldlier outlook in society at large was eroding the old imperative that the child should be brought up in a Godly household and prepared through catechization, rewards and punishment, for the salvation of its soul after death. Exhausted by religious wars and anxious to achieve a settled society after the Restoration of the Monarchy in 1688, the Whig government and the Anglican Church sought a more consensual rule and optimistic Christianity. Mercantile capitalism was expanding and commercial exchange demanded a liberal tolerance and a social demeanour of polished politeness towards other people of all ranks and classes. At this time John Locke published two important texts that were to dominate the history of educational ideas down to the present day: the *Essay Concerning Human Understanding* of 1690 and *Some Thoughts Concerning Education* of 1693.

In these widely read essays Locke famously articulated not only a consensual attitude to authority, whether in government or in the family, but a new imperative for a rational philosophy of mind based on liberal education of children. For in the new money economy of the rapidly commercializing society of the eighteenth century, the gentry and rising bourgeoisie became concerned not so much with spiritual salvation for their children but with their worldly opportunities. The fluctuations of the market in the new enterprise economy meant that prudent parents, who had some wealth, began to realize that the liberal education of their sons and daughters was almost as important to their worldly existence and status as their future inheritance. As modern sociologists have pointed out, the cultural capital of language, manners, orientations, connections and ways of thinking, form an inheritance far more enduring under capitalism than a material estate (Bourdieu and Passeron, 1977). Locke's readers understood that if a child's future station in life could be affected by his or her talents, manners and attitudes, then new relationships of dependence and affection needed to be forged within the family so that those attitudes were instilled before children grew to independence.

According to Locke, the child was not a diminutive adult but a tender infant without innate ideas or principles, 'a white paper void of all characters'. The great source of most of the ideas we have, he wrote, is the senses. 'The little, and almost insensible impressions on our tender infancies, have very important and lasting consequences'. 'All the Plays and Diversions of children should be directed towards good and useful Habits, or else they will introduce ill ones. Whatever they do leaves some impression on that tender Age, and from thence they receive a Tendency to Good or Evil' (Locke, 1693: 244).

Observing 'external sensible objects' conveys into the infant's mind distinct perceptions of things, according to the various ways those objects affected him or her. The other source from which experience furnishes the understanding with ideas is reflection. In time the child's mind reflects on 'its own operations about the ideas got by sensation', and thereby stores itself with a new set of ideas (Locke, 1693: 202). This central principle, that the young child learns through the early association of sensations and ideas, and then by reflecting, comparing, uniting and splitting them develops the ability to think in the abstract, still underlies child-centred educational thought. In the context of this active and sensory principle of learning Locke pointed again and again to the instinct to play, and to the liberty necessary for child autonomy and thus attentiveness:

> But to things we would have them learn, the great and only
> Discouragement I can observe is, that they are called to it; 'tis made
> their Business; they are teased and chid about it, and do it with
> Trembling and Apprehension, or when they come willing to it, are
> kept too long at it till they are quite tired: All of which intrenches too
> much on that natural freedom they extreamly affect. And 'tis that
> Liberty alone which gives the true Relish and Delight to their
> ordinary Play-Games. Turn the Tables, and you will soon find, they
> will soon change their Application ... (Locke, 1693: 116–17).

Hartley

In the mid-eighteenth century David Hartley further developed Locke's conceptualization of the learning mind. In his *Observations on Man, his Frame, his Duty and his Expectations* of 1749, Hartley adopted Newton's hypothesis that sensation was due to the vibrations of ether and small medullar particles resident in the pores of the nerves. Hartley pointed out that these nervous vibrations were communicated to the nerves of the brain, which, vibrating in their turn, produced tremors in the muscles which caused movements. Often called the 'Father of Psychology', Hartley explained that lesser vibrations in the brain, similar to those caused by actual sensations, could be caused by *ideas of* sensations. He concluded that every perception that entered the mind was inevitably linked with other impressions, which influenced the judgement either favourably or unpleasantly. As the individual is powerless to choose in what sequences any impression would be linked as it entered his or her mind, all judgements, as well as all affections, are, according to Hartley, determined from without. In other words, all early education helps to determine the moral outlook of the developing child.

Locke

The combined influence of Locke and Hartley's 'environmental' theories on educational thought has persisted to the present day. In the eighteenth century everyone interested in education read their texts. *Some Thoughts* itself appeared in at least twenty-five English, sixteen French, three German, six Italian, one Swedish, and two Dutch editions during the century. By mid century most learned commentators agreed that Locke's works were discussed throughout the literate population at large, while civil and religious liberty increasingly depended on Lockean principles. Numbers of articles in the *Spectator* and the *Tatler* and a host of more didactic works, widely disseminated Lockean ideas. Again and again throughout these texts Locke was invoked against severity and corporal punishment in favour of 'suppling' the child's will rather than 'breaking' it. Thus it was not only the vital importance of the infant's first impressions which made Locke's work so universally relevant to parents but his authoritative endorsement of more liberal ideas to do with governance and affect inside the family. 'I consider them as Children, who must be tenderly used', Locke wrote, 'who must play and have play-things' (Locke, 1693: 26). A gentle approach to the tender child would slowly correct him or her of the natural faults of childhood: 'Inadvertency, forgetfulness, unsteadiness, and wandering of Thought, are the natural Faults of childhood; and where therefore they are not observed to be wilful, are to be mentioned softly, and gain'd upon by time.' (Locke, 1693: 299).

Throughout the eighteenth century within wealthier families and in the families of the expanding groups of the 'middling sort', children were increasingly represented as tender and playful. Locke's claim, that by respecting children's instincts to play a more lasting educative influence could be brought to bear on them, helped to promote what was to become a vast new market of goods for children, such as toys and children's games. Throughout the century in provincial cities, as well as in London, printers began to produce well-printed and often illustrated children's books. By the end of the century the education of the young in most families with a little money now included educational toys such as dissected maps, cards, globes and natural history books, and family entertainment often included trips to lectures, museums, zoos, puppet shows, circuses and exhibitions of curiosities. In the new money economy of Britain's commercial society these shrewd parents had realized that Locke's liberal attitude to child-rearing was more conducive to their children's future creativity and enterprise, and hence their fortunes under the capitalist system, than a harsh and authoritarian upbringing which would school their offspring only for systems of tyranny and obedience.

THE GREAT CHILD-CENTRED GURU

Rousseau's Emile

One result of the fascination with education awakened by Locke was that many people took a deep interest in the writings of Rousseau. His work *Emile* of 1762 was widely read and discussed and its claims about the education of the virtuous citizen taken very seriously. It is a fictional account of a pupil who is in the care of a tutor who carefully arranges what is to be learned, all of which is determined by an understanding of the child's nature at each stage of his development. In *Emile*, Rousseau laid out a developmental schema of childhood that insisted on the 'natural' instincts of children and the ways the environment impacted on them.

> *We are born weak, we need strength; helpless, we need aid; foolish, we need reason. All that we lack at birth, all that we need when we come to man's estate, is the gift of education. This education comes to us from nature, from men, or from things. The inner growth of our organs and faculties is the education of nature, the use we learn to*

make of this growth is the education of men, what we gain by our experience of our surroundings is the education of things. Thus we are taught by three masters. If their teaching conflicts, the scholar is ill-educated and will never be at peace with himself; if their teaching agrees, he goes straight to his goal, he lives at peace with himself, he is well-educated. (Rousseau, 1762: 6)

Rousseau directly rebutted the idea of original sin by insisting that because children are made in the image of God, they are naturally good. Any corruption observable in the growing child could only be a result of social life. Consequently, Emile was to be reared in an isolated rural environment. In addition Rousseau insisted that children have different ways of seeing and understanding to those of adults, and they can only exercise reason on what is within their own experience and not on what is beyond it. In *Emile*, Rousseau postulates an ideal order of development of the male child that culminates in the realization of a 'true' self: one that avoids all the corruptions and artificialities of current society. 'To be something, to be himself, and always at one with himself, a man must act as he speaks, must know what course he ought to take, and must follow that course with vigour and persistence' (Rousseau, 1762: 6).

BUT WHAT OF GIRLS?

Famously, or rather infamously, Rousseau's insistence on naturalness and personal authenticity with its deep critique of society was only for *the boy child*. Central to Rousseau's theories was his openly expressed view that women were by nature different to men, comparatively lacking in rational potential and suited only to a rigorous training in domestic discipline. 'The search for abstract and speculative truths, for principles and axioms in science, for all that tends to wide generalisation, it is beyond a woman's grasp; their studies should be thoroughly practical' (Rousseau, 1762: 418).

The girl child's 'innate' female instincts are, he writes, only and entirely practical. Sophie, Emile's future wife and his model for all girl children, has only feelings of shame and modesty, the desire to please and an innate duplicity and cunning. To complement Emile and provide a source of moral strength for the male citizen, it was necessary, Rousseau insisted, for Sophie to be uneducated, trained only to suppress her weaker sexual self so as to become a devoted wife and mother within the natural institution of the family. Rousseau's schema was blatantly misogynist. Sophie should be trained also to attract men and understand and adapt to their passions. 'Woman, weak as she is and limited in her range of observation', wrote Rousseau, 'perceives and judges the forces at her disposal to supplement her weakness, and those forces are the passions of men' (Rousseau, 1762: 419). Nevertheless, his theme of the moral regeneration of the citizen through the influence of the family where he appeared to define and justify a vitally significant maternal role, confirming mothers as rulers of a separate domestic realm, was an attractive idea to many of his female readers.

Wollstonecraft However, despite Rousseau's dominating presence in educational child-centred historiography, recent feminist history has shown how leading contemporary women educationists, not only the conservatives Sarah Trimmer and Hannah More, but radical women such as Catharine Macaulay, Mary Wollstonecraft and Madame de Sevigny, who all believed in the project of widespread liberal education, were appalled by Rousseau's idea that this should only be confined to boys. Intellectual women both in Britain and France soon felt keenly that Rousseau's gendered argument – that Emile could only become an educated citizen *at the expense* of his female partner's independent moral and intellectual development – was deeply unjust, morally wrong and dangerous to civil society. A leading educationalist, Catherine Macaulay, wrote that Rousseau, potentially 'a man of genius' in idea of sexual difference and the subordination of women, lowered himself to a 'licentious pedant' (Macaulay, 1790: 206). In 1792 Mary Wollstonecraft published her passionate refutation of Rousseau's educational ideas, *A Vindication of the Rights of Woman*. In this breathtaking text she constructed a vision of the properly educated *female* child, which drew on the ideas of Locke and provided a powerful portrait of the young enlightened citizen, male or female – rational, caring, responsible and intellectual – sketching in this work an Enlightenment ideal that still resounds across the western world today.

> *Rousseau declares that a woman should never, for a moment, feel herself independent, that she should be governed by fear to exercise her natural cunning, and made a coquetish slave in order to render her a more alluring object of desire, a sweeter companion to man, whenever he chooses to relax himself. He carries the arguments,*

*which he pretends to draw from the indications of nature, still further
and insinuates that truth and fortitude, the corner stones of all
human virtue, should be cultivated with certain restrictions, because,
with respect to the female character, obedience is the grand lesson
which ought to be impressed with unrelenting rigour ... What
nonsense! ...*

*Were boys and girls permitted to pursue the same studies together,
those graceful decencies might be inculcated which produce modesty
without those sexual distinctions that taint the mind ... In short, in
whatever light I view the subject, reason and experience convince me
that the only method of leading women to fulfil their peculiar duties,
is to free them from all restraint by allowing them to participate in
the inherent rights of mankind.* (Wollstonecraft, 1792: 47)

By the end of the Enlightenment in the early nineteenth century,
as we shall see, two totally opposing views of the child had emerged
in European culture. In Britain, both these views were closely related
to the instinctive ideological values of different political parties. On
the one hand, conservatives still held to the old view that all children
were potentially sinful, and that the poor child was particularly at risk
of eternal damnation. This party held that only strict instruction in
the scriptures, mechanical discipline and constant surveillance would
rescue all children from the influence of the Devil and hence from
damnation to hell. On the other hand, liberals and radicals believed
almost exactly the opposite: that all children were born innocent,
that they had a subjectivity and a playfulness naturally given that
should be respected by the adults around them, especially those in
authority over them. Here history shows us the ways that the values
of the adults played out directly on child-rearing and educational
practices. We trace in this book the ways these opposing value systems resulted in a school system which was riven by unresolved tensions and oppositions – affecting the lives of countless teachers and
their young pupils. Thus we argue that values in a democratic nation
must be discussed and refined if we are to avoid some of the more
dreadful schooling practices suffered by children in the past. In this
story the idea of producing a young enlightened citizen who is curi-
ous, creative and autonomous, continually challenges the authoritarian instrumentalism of the conservative tradition.

THE STRUCTURE OF THIS BOOK

The main purpose of this book is to excavate from the past and articulate the submerged alternative, coherent set of child-centred values
that might help us look to the future. So rather than beginning with
practice, or even asking how we can improve practice (which often
leaves the underlying values untouched), we are suggesting we begin
with a set of beliefs and values that have formed a coherent enlightened view over the past three centuries and see if, by reclaiming this
particular view of the central ideas for education, we might be able
to offer an improved educational vision for the future. Ultimately, we
believe that in tracing the child-centred tradition from the Enlightenment, with its necessary liberal and creative elements, we demonstrate the need to reinstate more active, localized decisions and
judgements about the values and principles that all schools agree to
work to. The teacher and the school governor are key players in this
bid to enhance our children's education. In reinstating the exercise
of openly articulating professional decisions and judgements that
grow from values – personal beliefs, convictions, knowledge and
experience – values that are openly held and debated, universally
agreed and continually reviewed by teacher practitioners, we believe
that child-centredness would re-emerge as a crucial element of a
reformed, far more creative, education system.

Chapter 1 sets the scene for understanding the origins of child-centred education in the English Enlightenment and the ways educational ideas were developed in liberal circles at the end of the eighteenth century. Here the influence of the original leaders of the Industrial Revolution, the Birmingham Lunar Society, and their educational ideas and their family networks are brought to the fore. We examine the famous text *Practical Education*, published in 1798, by Richard Lovell Edgeworth and his daughter, the novelist Maria Edgeworth, who both belonged to this circle of friends, and who first set out a holistic and child-centred system of education. This opening chapter then moves to the counter-Enlightenment and looks at the origins and fortunes of the nineteenth-century infant school movement where the influence of Pestalozzi came to bear. Finally, the chapter moves to the mid-nineteenth century and examines Froebel's kindergarten movement that developed in Germany and spread across Britain, Europe and to many parts of the world, eventually influencing famous reformers such as Margaret McMillan, Susan Isaacs and John Dewey. We show the ways the kindergarten philosophy formalized and embodied many of the values of child-centredness that were extant in the British tradition.

In Chapter 2 we follow the child-centred tradition and the alternative instrumental and authoritarian ideology of the elementary and preparatory schools in the contrasting lives of two women teachers, Alice Berridge and Alice Hallouran, who both worked in education for many years in the twentieth century. Here we use oral testimony to explore the ways that personal values affect a lifetime of work in teaching. The chapter traces the deep ways that different versions of, and lives within, education are structured by different visions of civil society. In focusing on the lives of these two women we can trace the ways child-centred ideology of the Froebelian kindergarten movement spread and eventually flowered in the Hadow Report of 1931 and beyond as Britain struggled to liberalize its early childhood education for the poorest classes. We look at the ways the great issue of selection for secondary school, with a small proportion of children admitted to a different set of life chances in being admitted to grammar schools – first through the 'scholarship' examination and then, after the Second World War, the eleven-plus – kept child-centred education at bay. Through sensitive dialogue about their life histories with these two elderly former head teachers, women who gave their lives to the education of young children, the chapter traces, on the one hand, the ways that the constraints of the hegemony of the processes of selection for grammar school, the endless rigours of getting children through the eleven-plus, could become the rigid contours of a life spent in service to social mobility. On the other hand, a liberal progressive vision of the child could supply a life's dedication to, and embodiment of, a very different ideology in the period, carried out within the constrictions of poverty and incomprehension of teacher colleagues.

Chapter 3 completes this historical story by returning to the issue of selection for secondary school and the ways it militated against the child-centred vision enshrined in the Hadow Report, hopelessly destroying its effects despite the enthusiasm and creativity of many primary teachers and educationalists. The exigencies of selection for secondary school and the ways the eleven-plus could form and dictate the life chances of the growing child are reprised in considering the crucial effects the reform of secondary schools, the abolishing of grammar and secondary modern schools in the 1960s, had on primary education. Instituting comprehensive schools for all meant that the nation was freed at last from the exigencies of training for the eleven-plus and a progressive vision of education could finally flower in primary schools. The chapter examines the famous Plowden Report of 1967, its initial liberating effects on teacher and child creativity, and the subsequent attacks on its ideology, from the conservative Right in the notorious Black Papers of the early 1970s, and from the Marxist Left in accusations that it merely unleashed new methods of social control. The chapter goes on to outline the consistent ways this alternative tradition in education has been attacked, disappeared and falsely reinvoked in controversies over the nature of childhood and citizenship, finally examining the devastating redrawing of the primary curriculum more and more narrowly around assessment and measurement since 1988.

In our effort to construct a renewed model of child-centredness for the twenty-first century, in the next three chapters we consider in depth the philosophical principles and values that could form the core of a revived child-centred approach in schools. In Chapter 4 we first consider different interpretations of the idea of looking at the 'whole child' when we think of education in the child-centred tradition, focusing in particular on differing views of what constitutes personhood and personal autonomy. By evaluating different forms of *personhood*, the chapter argues for a particular view that centres on embodied, sensual and affectively rich thought rather than just the ability for rational or 'critical thinking', a new preoccupation. The chapter also explores the long-held child-centred belief that respect for the child involves consideration of the child as she or he is *in the present* more than a stress on what the child should become. We explore the implications of these views in terms of opportunities for agency and expression. The argument within this chapter finishes by suggesting that it is in this sense that the child-centred claim that 'the whole child' should be seen as at the centre of his or her education is best understood.

In Chapter 5 we continue this examination and new elaboration of the philosophy of the child-centred tradition, picking up themes from earlier chapters. We look briefly at the old child-centred claims, first raised by Locke, for 'active learning,' 'relevance' and 'interests', and move on to argue that a more fundamental value which lies behind these terms is captured by the notion of *meaning*. Learning which is genuinely felt as significant by a child will be the kind of learning which carries weight and meaning for that child. Ultimately, in this renewed tradition meaning is *the* prerequisite for coming to care and to feel passion about what we know and understand. The chapter argues that the current curriculum centres on knowledge and understanding that is layered *onto* children and largely neglects a child's need for passion, belief and conviction. As such, the curriculum does not offer knowledge that is sufficiently deep or robust to guide actions and choices for a way of living. We believe that the issue of *meaning* is more relevant and vital than any of the current remedies put forward to improve learning, including recent calls for 'personalization', 'inclusion' and 'individual needs'.

Chapter 6 focuses on one issue which is raised by notions of 'the whole child' and 'meaningful learning': the emphasis this appears to give to consideration of the individual. Here we argue to the contrary that one other vital strand has been the call for a communal nature to child-centred education, where collaborative and democratic learning experiences and the social construction of knowledge are seen as significant and of value. We explore this communal dimension of child-centredness and the chapter introduces and develops the notion of 'serious conversation'. This idea extends to the kind of conversations school can offer children within the practices and traditions in our heritage, as well as with their contemporary peers and teachers. The chapter subsequently explains the sense in which the social and moral dimensions of living are inextricably entwined with the personal and how the value of *relationship* therefore stands at the heart of child-centred education. As part of this argument, the ways and senses in which strong beliefs, passions and concerns are not simply individual acquisitions but can be (importantly for schools) acquired and generated through ethos and community are explored. How this rich version of interdependence highlights the fundamental importance of talk and goes some way to satisfying the demands of an active democracy are considered.

Finally, in Chapter 7 we discuss what essential reforms are needed for a new return to child-centredness in primary schools across the nation. However, our main point remains, that this tradition gives autonomy back to the historical actors within education – the teachers and children. Thus, we argue that there are no totalizing prescriptions for curriculum and school 'effectiveness', but rather we call for a renewed emphasis on child and adult creativity and suggest the kind of political will and decisions needed to allow that.

Thus, in setting out pictures from history and clear arguments for a particular view of education, we hope to provoke discussion in ways that will ensure that, whatever values come to be espoused in individual schools, they can become communally revived as living values, not just dry empty statements of intent. The whole-hearted holding of educational values as deeply as if they were personal is important in this view. We believe that if teachers are to live and work by a particular set of values, they need to be meaningful to them as individuals – to carry conviction and be something they care enough about to work with. However, particularly if this work is in a school, they need to be open, to be able to hone them in relation to others, and genuinely to collaborate in creating the value framework by which they will make decisions and view practice. Only in this way can an authentic and, we believe, desperately needed, child-centred vision re-emerge in the twenty-first century.

part I

THE CHILD-CENTRED LEGACY

chapter 1

THE ORIGINS OF CHILD-CENTRED EDUCATION

Throughout the eighteenth century Locke's ideas remained supreme for all those interested in education. In Britain's burgeoning commercial society his enlightened philosophy towards the young supported an enterprising and optimistic culture of progress that was to underpin technical invention in the Industrial Revolution. Many of the new middle classes became devoted to self-education and experimentation. Within this culture of scientific enterprise 'Literary and Philosophical' societies emerged. Difficulties of travel encouraged the formation of these local societies in nearly all the new industrial towns ands cities. Their members, men and women, were naturally interested in education and were concerned about ways and means of encouraging and supporting their children to read, discuss, experiment and invent. It was in late eighteenth-century Birmingham that the most famous of these societies flourished, one that was to bequeath a textual legacy of enlightenment, child-centred education to future generations.

THE LUNAR SOCIETY OF BIRMINGHAM

In 1765 a group of Birmingham men with a common interest in science and technology and a liberal and innovative mentality, came together to found the most famous and influential of these circles:

the Lunar Society of Birmingham. The founders were Matthew Boulton, a born promoter and improver, and his friend Erasmus Darwin (grandfather of Charles). Others included Glasgow's James Watt, who was interested in steam engines, James Keir, a leading industrial chemist, and John Whitehurst of Derby, a maker of clocks and scientific instruments with advanced ideas on electricity, meteorology, geology and steam engines. By 1775 they had been joined by Josiah Wedgwood, Richard Lovell Edgeworth and his friend the educational reformer, Thomas Day, and the renowned Unitarian Joseph Priestley. By the 1770s the group had established the practice of holding regular meetings at Boulton's house near Birmingham, in order to exchange information and test new ideas. They called themselves the 'Lunar Society' because they always met on Mondays nearest the full moon in order to get home by moonlight. This famous circle of thinkers and inventors continued to correspond and meet for years, and their families remained close for the rest of their lives, forming a long-lasting intellectual circle.

It is here, in the daily lives of the Lunar circle, that we can see the Enlightenment origins of child-centred education as a system, method and approach, for alongside their public projects that brought scientific knowledge to bear on an extraordinary number of industrial and social problems, the Lunar circle remained familial and domestic. Within their homes they developed their outstanding culture of education, observation, invention, and literary and philosophical critique. Indeed, the group's inventing and experimenting was intermingled with familial social practices: visiting, sharing information and theories, love affairs, advising on diseases and literary critique, much of it articulated in conversation and informal correspondence which often included drawings and poems. In all this daily round, children were involved, watching, listening, playing and experimenting for themselves.

Several younger members of these families eventually intermarried, carrying this intense domestic culture of scientific and intellectual learning into the Victorian period. It was members of the innovative Lunar circle that produced the most outstanding text on child-centred education, *Practical Education* by Richard Lovell Edgeworth and his daughter Maria.

The Edgeworths

As a young man Richard Lovell Edgeworth had developed an absorbing and inventive interest in mechanics and engineering, and this led him to make contact with members of the Lunar Society. He was to retain an intense and lasting interest in education throughout his life, particularly home education, as he married four times and in total fathered 21 live children. His first wife died in 1778, which meant that he had to take care of 5-year-old Maria, her older brother, and two younger sisters. Soon afterwards he married Honora Sneyd of Lichfield, with whom he produced two more children. Honora died in 1780 and in the following year Richard Lovell Edgeworth married her sister Elizabeth, with whom he produced a further nine children. In 1782 the Edgeworth family returned to Edgeworthstown in Ireland. Elizabeth died in 1797 and one year later he married his fourth wife, Frances Beaumont, with whom he had six more children. Over these years Richard Lovell Edgeworth devoted himself to managing and improving his estate, dabbling in Irish politics, continuing his experiments and inventions, and above all, working at educating his numerous children. His own mother had been a believer in the educational ideas of Locke and she had taught Richard Lovell Edgeworth herself, encouraging in him both an independence of mind and a fascination with empirical observation and experiment. As his children grew up in the large house at Edgeworthstown he fostered this same independence of

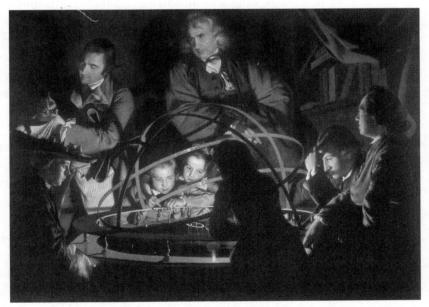

Joseph Wright of Derby, The Orrery. Wright was friendly with, and often painted, members of the Lunar Society. Here we can see children and adults learning together through active engagement in scientific wonder. Reproduced with the permission of the trustees of Derby Museums.

mind in his numerous progeny. His older daughter, Maria, became an outstanding writer. By the end of the century Maria was a renowned novelist, her works much admired by most intellectual readers of her day, including the still obscure Jane Austen. Nevertheless it was the day-to-day necessity of educating a large household of children that prompted Richard Lovell Edgeworth and Maria to produce a full-scale educational course. Together they wrote the most comprehensive and child-centred educational treatise of the period, *Practical Education*, a quarto work of 775 pages full of example and precept, published in 1798.

PRACTICAL EDUCATION

Practical Education begins with early childhood priorities such as playing with toys, performing simple tasks and instilling obedience and truthfulness. Then come exact recommendations for teaching particular subjects such as English grammar, classical literature, geography, mechanics and chemistry. The final sections address the development of the child's faculties and include chapters on memory and invention, taste and imagination, wit and judgement. The two Edgeworths, father and daughter, were close adherents to Locke's principles. Working closely in their child-filled domestic setting, they both also belonged to wider scientific and intellectual circles. So, although based on Lockean principles of childhood freedom, active learning and respect for the developing intellect of the growing child, they also carefully integrated theories and scientific ideas from the Lunar circle and progressive continental intellectuals.

Based originally on Lockean principles, and incorporating a century of natural philosophical ideas, *Practical Education* was the first educational work to fully configure an experimental and holistic method of 'discovery' in education. Indeed, Richard Lovell Edgeworth's fascination with empirical observation and experiment suffuses much of the text. Although it was designed for middle-ranking and elite families, in its pages we can trace a direct route back from our child-centred ideas to their Enlightenment origins. As the historian Brian Simon has pointed out, instead of providing children with artificial and expensive imitative toys, such as dolls' houses and tea sets, the Edgeworths insist that they should have card, pasteboard, scissors, wire, gum and wax. Children should be encouraged, they wrote, to find things out for themselves, to make models illustrating mechanical principles and to undertake a range of chemical and physical experiments. Young learners should be given small stills, tea kettles and lamps for boiling, distilling and subliming. They should be expected to collect and fill their shelves with natural objects such as shells and ores logically arranged. Cheap microscopes should be provided and the learners encouraged to carry out experiments in optics. All manner of carpenter's tools should also be available, also models of machines and instruments that can be taken apart. Experiments in chemistry should be conducted with simple household equipment. Above all, in place of showing to children the steps of a discovery, they should be given time to invent and discover for themselves (Simon, 1960).

Again and again the Edgeworths refer to the centrality of the child's active play to the learning mind:

> When a pedantic schoolmaster sees a boy eagerly watching a paper kite, he observes 'What a pity it is that children cannot be made to mind their grammar as well as their kites!' A man of sense will see the same sight with a different eye; in this pernicious love of play he will discern the symptoms of a love of science, and, instead of deploring the natural idleness of children, he will admire the activity which they display in the pursuit of knowledge. (Edgeworth and Edgeworth, 1798: 30)

Several chapters explain particular ways in which children can be encouraged to learn through invention rather than being made to learn by rote through enforced discipline or instructed in facts beyond their comprehension. Children should not only be allowed to experiment, insist the Edgeworths, but to think freely without interference. 'To win the attention of vivacious children we must sometimes follow them in their zigzag course, and even press them to the end of their train of thought' they wrote (Edgeworth and Edgeworth, 1798: 99). Hence children's attention, interest and understanding should be awakened by sympathy. Beyond this nurturing of scientific curiosity, invention and experiment, the Edgeworths set out the best principles of acquiring and using language, and they discuss ways of mastering the symbolic systems involved in reading, arithmetic, writing and spelling. Child memory should be developed by 'well arranged associations' and the method of instruction genuinely conversational, that is, through democratic dialogue between kindly teacher and autonomous learner. Correspondingly, the Edge-worths have no time for showy accomplishments in children, believ-ing that true learning produces sober rational sense. The latter quality is illustrated in *Practical Education* by a variety of small anec-dotes and stories from their archive of experiences within the Edge-worth family. Visitors to Edgeworthstown House certainly seemed to have been impressed by the Edgeworth children, whose articulacy and enthusiasm in conversing about ideas were much admired.

Practical Education is a corner stone in the history of child-centred education. In bringing a century of Enlightenment ideas to the education of the young, not only did they ingeniously promote con-temporary science, but they displayed a sophisticated sense of the young mind, and the ways imagination and autonomy support solid learning. Most importantly, *Practical Education* consistently con-structs an adult–child relationship based on mutual respect, reason and justice. As they wrote:

> *Young people, who find that their daily pleasures depend not so much upon their own exertions as upon the humour and caprice of others, become courtiers; they practice all the arts of persuasion, and all the crouching hypocrisy which can deprecate wrath or propitiate favour. Their notions of right and wrong cannot be enlarged; their recollection of the rewards and punishments of childhood are always connected with ideas of tyranny and slavery; and when they break their own chains, they are impatient to impose similar bonds upon their inferiors.* (Edgeworth and Edgeworth, 1798: 244).

When *Practical Education* first appeared it met with great approval by leading educationalists. It was recognized 'as the most ingenious and useful treatise on a very important subject'. Clearly the enlight-ened intelligentsia who bought the book were shown how children, boys and girls, need to be nurtured within the educated family, they were taught how children learned through experiment, play and invention, and most importantly they were reminded constantly that children developed their intellects through reading and democratic discussion with adult members of their family communities. 'Edge-worthian' educational culture was to be quietly sustained in many leading families throughout the first anxious and religious decades of the early nineteenth century.

EDUCATION IN THE COUNTER-ENLIGHTENMENT

By the time *Practical Education* was published at end of the eighteenth century the English Enlightenment was coming to a close. The French Revolution of 1789, at first welcomed by the liberal-minded as a new dawn, had dissolved into the revolutionary 'Terror'. By 1793 the British were at war with Napoleonic France. By the beginning of the nineteenth century the problems of the British nation had become unanswerable and unstoppable: starvation, unrest and exploitation for the increasing numbers of dispossessed poor, and the frightening possibility of revolution for the middle and upper classes. In rural areas enclosures meant that many of the poor became redundant and families made their ways to the nearest towns to find work in the factories. As the factory system developed and industry grew, vast tracts of slums containing unprecedented numbers of rest- less and scarcely governable masses of poor people spread out around the industrial towns and cities. There were children everywhere. It is estimated that by 1810 over 50 per cent of the population was under 20 years of age and most of them were under the age of 10. The poor now provided a constant threat of revolution and their filth and degradation a constant reproach to those with enlightenment values.

Bell and Lancaster   Educational discussion among the governing classes changed inexorably from a polite consideration of enlightened practices within the genteel family to new anxieties and solutions to the prob- lems of irreligion, degradation and 'Jacobin' propaganda among the ever-increasing numbers of the poor. One solution, hotly debated as to who had invented it, was the monitorial school. Holding to an image of a machine, the Anglican, Andrew Bell, and the Quaker, Joseph Lancaster, both came up with the idea of huge schools for the poor where the many children would teach each other. Vast numbers of young were organized into small groups of five or six where they were instructed by another child, a 'monitor' who taught them to read by working through words on cards. The whole human machine depended on finely worked out systems of rewards and punishments. Each learner learnt the words by rote, and sufficient mastery enabled them to become monitors themselves, instructed in turn by the mas- ter. In the early decades of the century the machine-like quality of these schools impressed observers of all religious and political per- suasions. Monitorial schools sprang up across the country and the children of the poor were herded in. It was several decades before the basic ineffectuality of the method was exposed and the schools fell into disrepute.

In fact there was a huge variety of schools in the early nineteenth century with little or no state support. Alongside the monitorial schools some of the old eighteenth-century subscription charity schools carried on their work. By now they had become distinct and respectable day schools, attended not by the very poor but by the children of artisans and shopkeepers, the girls destined to become upper servants in gentry households and the boys artisans and factory managers. Sunday schools, the large ones situated in industrial areas and taking in huge numbers of children who worked all week in the factories, had grown to enormous numbers. They were no longer entirely under the auspices of the Anglican Church, as many were founded and run by Dissenters with teachers from local humble communities. Parish schools, instituted by the British and Foreign Society and the National Society, existed alongside thousands of practically invisible dame schools. In these one woman took in a handful of children to her own home and taught them to read alongside carrying out domestic chores, all of this helped to spread and maintain literacy levels among the poor. In the towns and cities 'ragged' schools were started for those children who were simply too poor to attend other kinds of schools.

Among this educational chaos of the first half of the century, government initiatives were hopelessly riven by theological dispute. Deep differences existed between members of the Anglican Church and various sects of Dissenters that prevented the establishment of a centralized system of teacher training, curriculum development, payment of teachers and the building of schools until well into the 1850s. Yet despite the terrible exploitation, starvation and disease suffered by the industrial poor and the many strictures laid on them in vast numbers of monitorial, Sunday and charity schools, in textbooks, tracts, stories, handbooks, and sermons, a progressive, child-centred vision remained. Many of those reared in more affluent Victorian families admired 'Edgeworthian' educational ideas (including the young Queen herself who had loved Maria Edgeworth's educational tales as a child). It was often members of these more 'enlightened' families who were anxious to carry these ideas to the poor and outcast. Scientific, often dissenting families, particularly those descended from eighteenth-century Rational Dissent – now called Unitarians – brought their reforming instincts and belief in human progress to the terrible problems of the poor. Societies were formed and subscriptions raised. Among the more child-centred, the ideas of Johann Pestalozzi were often discussed and valued.

PESTALOZZI

Pestalozzi   Johann Pestalozzi had run a series of schools for the rural poor in his native Switzerland, bringing to them his own sense that children were unique and that their understandings unfolded in an atmosphere of kindly approbation. He developed his own 'science' of education, based on Locke and Hartley. He believed that consciousness was developed first by perceiving and considering objects, and from them the child slowly developed the abstract systems of reading and arithmetic through counting and measuring. Richard Lovell Edgeworth had visited him in his school in Switzerland in 1812 and Maria Edgeworth returned there after the death of her father in 1817. Nearly all these educationists and reformers were impressed by Pestalozzi's warmth, his devotion to children and his view that the liberal education of the poor could have desirable political consequences beyond the small society of the school. Pestalozzi held to the philosophical view of the child's innate wisdom. This, he argued, must be nurtured sympathetically in all children as consciousness unfolded. Moral education, first developed instinctively between mother and child, slowly merges into intellectual education, which must first be centred on the perception of objects and then adapted and expanded as the mind expands. His ideas attracted all reformers who wished to move education away from its focused concentration on rote memorization and instruction, the ubiquitous and ineffectual pedagogy of the age. His vision of all children as active learners, so that the task of educators is not to instruct but to stimulate self-activity through the training of the senses, is perhaps Pestalozzi's most lasting contribution to educational philosophy.

THE NINETEENTH-CENTURY INFANT SCHOOLS

In 1836, a group of leading Evangelicals decided that infant education in England must be taken in hand. Although there had been an infant school movement earlier in the century, it had all but died away and very young children, up to the age of 7, being now debarred by law from working in the factories, were usually left idle on the streets in the industrial ghettos or in the rough and often neglectful care of poor older women. As a result the evangelical Home and Colonial Infant School Society was founded to establish schools and to train infant teachers. Predictably the evangelical members of the Home and Colonial Society saw the child as a sinner who needed to be saved rather than an innocent being whose unfolding conscious-ness required a sympathetic and enriching environment. The founders of Home and Colonial set out to bring the memorization of Biblical knowledge and the mechanical routines of the monitorial schools to infant education.

Wordsworth   However, the members of the Society soon found that it could not in any serious way ignore or repudiate the child-centred tradition now widely endorsed in those parts of society interested in education of the poor. Many leading educationalists now adhered to a 'Pestalozzian' faith in creating a moral, developmentally aware and active pedagogy for all young children. The intensely written and widely read works of the Romantic poets, chiefly those of Wordsworth, contributed to this incoherent but crucial faith in childhood innocence and subjectivity. Forty years before, in *The Prelude*, Wordsworth had laid down a lasting template of child innocence in his famous *Immortality Ode*. It contains perhaps the finest Romantic justification and celebration of the unique vision of the child:

> *Our birth is but a sleep and a forgetting:*
> *The soul that rises with us, our life's star,*
> *Hath had elsewhere its setting,*
> *And cometh from afar;*
> *Not in entire forgetfulness,*
> *And not in utter nakedness,*
> *But trailing clouds of glory do we come*
> *From God, who is our home.* (Wordsworth, *The Prelude*, 1805).

Wordsworth's poetry was deeply admired and extremely popular in the early Victorian period. He was still alive, and mixed with some of the most important educational and social reformers of his day, many of whom, believing in his vision of childhood innocence, and his sense of a common humanity, loyally called themselves 'Wordsworthians'.

Soon the Home and Colonial was forced to recognize the deep-rootedness of the British child-centred tradition in infant education.

The importance of love in moral education, the focus on the stimulation of the child's natural curiosity and activity, and the vital instilling of habits of observation, meant that lessons on objects and toys, the use of coloured pictures, instruction in natural history, use of practical materials such as beans and rags which introduced ideas of form, colour and number, freedom and exercise in the playground (seen as the laboratory of character and an important point of contact with the natural world) all became adopted in the Home and Colonial infant teacher training programme.

Carpenter

By the mid-century, reformers such as Mary Carpenter, sister-in-law of the novelist Elizabeth Gaskell, directed the attention of the reading public to the necessity of education rather than jail sentences for 'juvenile delinquents' from the 'poor and perishing' classes. Carpenter tirelessly ran ragged and reformatory schools herself. Her teaching journal and subsequent books on the education of the poorest children of 1850 show her devotion to Locke's environmental ideas and the reforming possibilities of gentle and child-centred education. 'Were there not an indestructible germ of a divine nature in these unhappy little beings, their case would indeed be hopeless; they must be first lured to school, and patiently borne with for many a toilsome hour and long day, before the seed of life perceptibly springs up'. (Carpenter, 1853: 52)

Dickens

Nevertheless, numerous infant and monitorial schools still held to the practice of biblical memorization, mechanical drills and impersonal systems of discipline as the only ways of 'managing' large numbers of the young poor. Charles Dickens famously entered the reforming lists with his attack on mindless rote learning in Gradgrind's school for the industrial poor. In *Hard Times* the sheer pointlessness of authoritarian school teaching is cleverly parodied. In Gradgrind's class, the boy Bitzer eagerly and relentlessly mouths rote-learnt verbiage in his description of a horse. 'Quadruped. Gramnivorous. Forty teeth, namely twenty-four grinders, four eye-teeth, and twelve incisive. Sheds coat in spring; in marshy countries, sheds hoofs, too. Hoofs hard, but requiring to be shod with iron. Age known by marks in mouth.' (Dickens, 1854: 4)

Risibly, and yet poignantly, while Bitzer is regarded as an educational success, his classmate Sissy Jupes, 'girl number twenty', who actually works with horses, is far too inhibited by the school system to 'define a horse'. However, despite Dickens's attack, and even the official dissatisfaction with the observable hopelessness of such pedagogic methods in British schools, including government inspection reports that confirmed their futility, the nation continued to cling to an authoritarian approach, with mechanical drills and rote learning for vast numbers of children. By the 1850s, however, a new educational philosophy had arrived in Britain, which was to finally establish child-centred education on a wide-ranging and powerful institutional base. The kindergarten movement was to grow and challenge the ideology and formal approach of much state-funded education up to the present day.

THE INVENTION OF THE KINDERGARTEN

Froebel

Perhaps the most powerful institutional framework ever invented to embody and promote child-centred ideas was the *kindergarten* invented by Friedrich Froebel. Although simply a small-time 'alternative' educationist from Prussia, Froebel developed his philosophy of education in ways that finally and completely fused child-centred theory and method together into a complete system of education for young children which could be carried out in schools. What were Froebel's principles? Froebel had worked with Pestalozzi but he became convinced that everything functions in relation to God, the total Unity, yet each self has its own purpose that needs fulfilment here and now. After the Napoleonic wars Froebel's older brothers sent him their sons to educate. He bought an old derelict farm in Keilhau in 1817 and set up a school where he could put his ideas into practice. In 1836 Froebel began the project that occupied him till his death in 1852. Working from his philosophy of the unity of all things, he began to focus on the natural instincts and play of the young child. He was convinced that adults should not ignore this play – as (he believed) had been the case in all educational systems until Pestalozzi – but should *foster* it. In fact it was in the old Lockean vein that Froebel insisted that only by the extension and enrichment of the child's instinct to involve itself in active play could sympathetic adult educators help the child in his or her full development as an 'acting, feeling, and thinking' human being.

At Blankenburg, a few miles from Keilhau, Froebel fully developed his 'early childhood pedagogics'. He designed soft woollen balls, wooden bricks, balls, prisms and cylinders, cut-outs made from cardboard and wooden frames for weaving, all of which came to be known as 'Froebel's gifts and occupations'. He then created an industrial enterprise called The Institute for the Fostering of the Creative Activity Drive to make the gifts and print the explanations and instructions. Through the production and distribution of these educational materials his ideas began to spread. His greatest success was in Dresden where Dr Peters, the mathematics teacher at the Dresden Gymnasium, saw a mathematical potential in the gifts. Despite attacks by the clergy and conservative teacher training instructors, more and more parents expressed interest in his system. For several years Froebel searched for the right name to give his early childhood pedagogy. The fostering of the child's natural instincts implied understanding its growth, guarding and cultivating it like a good gardener tending a young plant. The name 'kindergarten' came to him like a 'revelation' and the first kindergarten was officially opened in Blankenburg in 1840. Again there are powerful echoes here of Locke's 'little garden plots' and a renewed faith in Locke's and Rousseau's assertion of the inner and inescapable development of 'child nature'.

Froebel then began to develop a further dimension to his pedagogical system. He realized that much of children's play activity is culturally based. Children naturally mimic, sing, dance and listen to stories from the social world around them. His system of enriched activity needed to encompass these activities. Between 1840 and 1844 he worked to produce his *Mother Song Book*. He had observed, recorded and collected a variety of children's games and songs over a long period. Working with two young artists from Keilhau community, the music teacher Kohl and the art teacher Unger, he created an illustrated book of songs with accompanying finger actions for the child. Froebel then turned his mind to what would become the most powerful political element in his ideas, the central role of women in his educational process. In a letter to 'The Women of Blankenburg' in 1839 he asked them to form women's associations which would help them study the successful development of pre-school children. Here women would discuss their observations of their own children and relate these to his new educational ideas. More importantly, they would encourage the training of young women so that more kindergartens could be established. Froebel went on lecture tours, concentrating on the establishment of kindergartens and women's associations.

THE KINDERGARTEN COMES TO BRITAIN

Marenholtz-Bulow

It was a courageous German aristocrat, the Baroness Bertha Von Marenholtz-Bulow, who was chiefly responsible for spreading the philosophy of the kindergarten all over Europe by travelling to Britain, France, Italy, and then corresponding and networking with teachers from many parts of the world. The indefatigable Baroness, who was estranged from her husband and who had lost her own delicate son at 21, as a result, she believed, of his harsh upbringing forced on him by his aristocratic father, spent the rest of her life devoted to proselytizing Frobel's child-centred system. The Baroness was openly critical of society in these modern industrializing countries and believed passionately that only a more child-centred education of the young would achieve reform.

> The child like simplicity which surrenders itself to a higher and invisible power is now almost unknown, for its source in the original unsullied nature of childhood becomes early corrupted, and education directs the mind only to outward things: learning has become to be little more than acceptance of what is imparted, leaving no room for any original material to come to the surface, and stifling the innate faculties ... And because this is the case we see everywhere restlessness, discontent, a piteous seeking for unattained happiness – a deep vein of sadness runs through modern society ... (Marenholtz-Bulow, 1868: 47).

Here in her works on Froebel's theories we can see the way his ideas tapped into common contemporary anxieties about the nature of childhood, its necessary freedom and activity, and the price paid for its harsh neglect. 'A right education' she insists, 'consists in so strengthening and encouraging all the natural dispositions of a child that they conduce to the end which nature has set before them'. (Marenholtz-Bulow, 1868: 27)

> The play of children is for them, at the same time, work, for it serves to develop their members, senses, organs. After the first unregulated feeling and grasping of their little hands, their favourite occupation is to dabble in some soft mess – earth, sand or what not – and to try their skill at shaping and producing. Modelling is one of the first necessities of child nature. But even this instinct if left to itself will

lead to no end: education must supply the material and guidance necessary for its development, and must convert the aimless touching and fumbling into systematic construction, and direct the mere instinct into a channel of useful activity, all of which is done in the Kindergarten. (Marenholtz-Bulow, 1868: 29)

Ronge

The first English kindergarten was established by her compatriot Bertha Meyer, daughter of a wealthy businessman and a divorcee with four children, who had married Johannes Ronge in 1850 when they both left Germany for England. Bertha Meyer was an energetic and enthusiastic disciple of Froebel. In Hamburg in 1849 she and a number of friends had engaged Froebel to live with them for a period of six months to teach them his philosophy and methods before they all went off to different parts of Germany to set up kindergartens for themselves. When the Ronges arrived in England they settled first in Hampstead, where they set up a kindergarten, and then moved to Tavistock Place in 1854. Here Froebel's games, songs and occupations kept children between the ages of three and seven orderly, healthy, busy and creative, and drew admiring visitors. In 1855 Bertha Ronge, (with her husband's name also upon it to add authority) published her important manual, *A Practical Guide to the English Kindergarten.*

In her *Practical Guide*, first Ronge insists on a deep sensitivity of mind in all young children, 'the more tender the age of children, the more important is their development, because impressions are then more deep and lasting', a fact she believed was dangerously ignored in English education. Yet indigenous writers, as we have seen from Locke and Hartley onwards, had expressed this very idea. Unconsciously repeating the arguments of the Edgeworths in their section on toys in *Practical Education*, Ronge exclaims:

look into the nurseries and see how the children are generally treated ... The toy shops have supplied every variety of dolls, animals, houses etc. but they are finished materials, and the child can only look at them or use them in a given form in imitiation of the ideas of others. However the child, by the very impulse of his nature, wants to create; and as he finds nothing to represent his own ideas, he destroys the dolls, drums, boxes, and scatters the remains about the room. (Ronge and Ronge, 1855: v)

Just like the Edgeworths, the Ronges insist on the creative activity of the child. In this case Froebel, they insist, has supplied a range of games and occupations that integrate the active playfulness of the child:

> The games are so organised that all the faculties are harmoniously developed, and that play is not a mere external amusement, but a means of culture and a useful labour for the child ... Froebel supplied the children with material, with which, as will be seen from the description of the various Gifts, the children can produce an unlimited number of forms. (Ronge and Ronge, 1855: v)

The *Practical Guide* goes on to describe, with great thoroughness, an enormous number of forms and ideas made possible by rearrangements of the wooden cubes and blocks of Froebel's 'gifts'. Mathematical ideas, mainly fractions, are derived from the different configurations, but the little wooden bricks and blocks are also used to express material objects, stories and ideas. The *Practical Guide* then turns attention to describing the variations and possibilities of Froebel's 'occupations'. These consist of stick-laying, three-dimensional shape-making by joining sticks with soft peas, paper-plaiting, paper folding and cutting, painting and clay modelling. The *Practical Guide* is fulsomely illustrated and exhaustively detailed.

The Pigeon House

Illustration from Bertha Ronge's Practical Guide to the English Kinder Garten *reproduced by permission of the Syndics of Cambridge University Library. Froebel's Pigeon House Game shows the spirit of active learning through bodily play.*

The kindergarten movement continued to grow and flourish throughout Britain and the rest of Europe, Russia, America, then India and other parts of the world. In 1857 the Ronges visited Manchester where they helped to form the Manchester Committee for the Extension of the Kindergarten System. Several German teachers resident in Manchester helped to found kindergartens there. In 1873 the Manchester Froebel Society was formed, followed by a similar society in London in 1874, and the Home and Colonial Infant School Society officially changed its Pestalozzian principles for Froebelian ones in the 1860s. These were all incorporated into the National Froebel Union in 1893.

As the nineteenth century came to a close there now existed two distinct and opposing educational ideologies in Britain. On the one hand as we have seen, stretching from the Enlightenment origins of Locke and Hartley, passed down to posterity through the Edgeworths' famous *Practical Education*, influenced by the continental educationalists Pestalozzi and Froebel, the kindergarten now offered a child-centred curriculum, where play and experimentation, gardening and singing formed the child's day. Much of the children's time was spent forming patterns and making models to their own designs using Froebel's specially invented gifts and occupations. On the other hand, as we shall see, huge schools were being built for the young poor that continued to offer regimentation, rote learning, and authoritarian methods, increasingly combined and controlled by proliferating forms of measured standards.

FURTHER READING

Butler, M. (1972) *Maria Edgeworth: A Literary Biography*. Oxford: Clarendon Press.

Edgeworth, M. and Edgeworth, R.L. (1798) *Practical Education*. London: J. Johnson.

Liebschner, J. (1991) *The Foundations of Progressive Education*. Cambridge: Lutterworth Press.

Liebschner, J. (1992) *A Child's Work: Freedom and Play in Froebel's Educational Theory and Practice*. Cambridge: Lutterworth Press.

Locke, J. (1690) *An Essay Concerning Human Understanding*. London.

Locke, J. (1693) *Some Thoughts Concerning Education*. London; edited with introduction and notes by R.H. Quick, Cambridge, 1880.

Manton, J. (1976) *Mary Carpenter and the Children of the Streets.* London: Heinemann.

Pestalozzi, J.H. (1900) *How Gertrude Teaches her Children.* Trans. E. Cooke. 2 edn. London.

Ronge, B. and Ronge, J. (1855) *A Practical Guide to the English Kindergarten: Being an Exposition of Froebel's System.* London.

Rousseau, J.-J. (1762) *Emilius and Sophia: or, a new system of education.* Translated by William Kenrick. London.

Schofield, R. (1963) *The Lunar Society of Birmingham: A Social History of Provincial Science and Industry in Eighteenth-Century England.* Oxford: Clarendon Press.

chapter 2

CONTRASTING VISIONS: CONTRASTING LIVES

ELEMENTARY SCHOOLS FOR ALL

Where did child-centred teaching go in the face of the onslaught of numbers of the industrial poor? After 1870 when state education officially became free, secular, and compulsory, new schools were built with classrooms designed to take an *average* of 60 children, rising to 80 children in infant departments. Here the received theory of teaching required the imposition upon the schoolroom of the teacher's commanding presence. The desks were heavy and often fixed to the floor and the pupils all faced the teacher at the front. Reports and memoirs show that these conditions resulted in a perpetual strain on the organization, the voice, the temper and physique of the teacher. In these schools, as one commentator put it, 'class discipline could only be maintained by great strictness and perpetual vigilance'. However, there were certain methods and practices that helped control these large numbers of potentially unruly children. Indeed, throughout the nineteenth century, with the growth of institutions such as schools, prisons and hospitals a whole set of procedures had been carefully developed to help control, measure and train individuals in the system so that they would not and could not resist authority. In the huge elementary schools it was essential to render the children docile so that a relatively young man or woman could order and instruct such large numbers. Despite the perpetual shouting and the occasional beatings of older children, it was soon discovered that the process of setting standards and examining children in them helped enormously with classroom control.

Foucault

As the philosopher Michael Foucault has so brilliantly pointed out in his book on new forms of surveillance and control in the nineteenth-century city, *Discipline and Punish*, examinations formalize and document in writing the position of the individual in a hierarchy, and make it possible to determine categories and fix norms (Foucault, 1977). Within the elementary schools the examination process could reduce the individual to a series of fixed features, making it possible to build an almost mechanical system of pedagogy resting on anonymous relations of disciplinary power through grouping and setting, testing and grading of child pupils. Since the introduction of the Revised Code in 1861 the elementary school curriculum had been organized according to 'Standards'. This meant mixed-aged classes of children grouped according to their attainment in up to seven standards (different levels in reading, writing, arithmetic and needlework for girls.) Inspectors noticed how effective the 'Standards' examination was in checking, prompting, copying and constraining the uneasy shifting from place to place by the children. Indeed, the examination was so helpful in maintaining control over unruliness that extra tests were added to the system, so that in addition to the annual government examination there was a similar individual test, given by the school Board inspector, halfway through the school year. Preparation for these examinations monopolized the labours of both teachers and children throughout the year. Government grants were paid to the schools on the basis of examinations set and administered by the Education Department, the infamous 'payment by results'.

However, in the teeth of this widespread disciplinary pedagogy, the kindergarten movement was becoming more confidently established, confirming a more liberal and intellectual view of childhood. The first kindergartens formed in London and Manchester attracted the attention of many women teachers in England. By 1874 the Froebel Society had been formed, which translated his writings into English, published its own pamphlets and set up training institutions to provide training for kindergarten teachers. By the end of the nineteenth century hundreds of trained teachers were working in kindergartens, private and public, and the Education Department had recognized in elementary schools teachers possessing the National

Froebel Union Certificate. There is no doubt that all this networking and educational activity slowly affected the state's infant schools. The nation was slowly coming to accept that young children, all children – up to the age of 7 – should have a 'childhood'.

Froebelianism

As we have seen, the ideology of Froebelianism, worked out through its child-centred practices inside the Froebel colleges and kindergartens, was in almost total contradiction to that of nineteenth-century elementary school orthodoxy. In place of the docility of the body of the child there was active freedom of movement. In place of hierarchical observation there was trusted playfulness. In place of the fostering of teacher authority through tests and examinations, documentation, standards and competitiveness, there was wide-ranging individualization, culture of the children's personalities, and promotion of active creativity. Slowly these ideals and practices began to challenge not only the pedagogy of the state infant schools but also the methods of teaching the older children in elementary schools, that is, the education of children aged 7–11. Thus the 'new education' was no longer confined to the kindergarten. The ideals of self-activity, freedom of movement, space, a garden and communal play and work were now beginning to seem the best for all children. 'Progressivism', as this form of child-centred education was now called, began to undermine the old orthodoxy before the First World War and in the 1920s it flourished, particularly in the teacher training colleges. Influential educationalists such as Margaret McMillan and Susan Isaacs in Britain and John Dewey in America added intellectual weight to this child-centred educational tradition.

The Hadow Report

In the 1920s and 1930s several of the famous Hadow Reports confirmed the vital importance of a more a liberal and child-centred approach in English primary schools. Altogether, the Hadow Committee published three very important reports affecting primary-aged children, in 1926, 1931 and 1933, all of which led to major changes in the structure of primary education. In particular, they resulted in separate and distinctive educational practice for children aged 5–7 years, and 7–11 years. For both these groups of children, an educational style which emphasised a more child-centred approach was recommended to replace the more didactic and syllabus-centred approach which still typified practice in the elementary schools. In the words of the Hadow Report of 1931, for the education of children aged broadly 5–11 years:

The schools, feeling that what they can do best is the old familiar business of imparting knowledge, have reached a high level of technique in that part of their functions, but have not clearly grasped its proper relation to the whole. In short, while there is plenty of teaching which is good in the abstract, there is too little which helps children directly to strengthen and enlarge their instinctive hold on the conditions of life by enriching, illuminating and giving point to their growing experience.

Applying these considerations to the problem before us, we see that the curriculum is to be thought of in terms of activity and experience rather than of knowledge to be acquired and facts to be stored. Its aim should be to develop in a child the fundamental human powers and to awaken him to the fundamental interests of civilised life so far as these powers and interests lie within the compass of childhood, to encourage him to attain gradually to that control and orderly management of his energies, impulses and emotions, which is the essence of moral and intellectual discipline, to help him to discover the idea of duty and to ensue it, and to open out his imagination and his sympathies in such a way that he may be prepared to understand and to follow in later years the highest examples of excellence in life and conduct. (Hadow Report, 1931: 74, 75)

SECONDARY EDUCATION FOR ALL

The trouble was that, as pressure grew in the 1920s to allow more children to progress into a secondary school, the processes of selection became sharpened. For all primary schools, however child-centred their intentions, the great issue loomed of the 'scholarship' examination at age 11. This competitive examination kept the curriculum for primary school children in a straitjacket. Many adults still remember the formal teaching, the streaming and grooming that went on in school in the years before they were 11 years of age. If, for Froebelians, childhood was going to be a time of careful nurture, of play and of democratic and creative freedom, then all the child's future chances in the world of education and beyond must not hang on what was to them the epitome of repressive social technology – a competitive examination.

After the Second World War the battle over selection at age 11 deepened and intensified. The Butler Act of 1944 had divided the nation into three groups of children: the 'gold children', who went forward to the local grammar school (between about 12 per cent and 20 per cent), the 'silver children', about 10 per cent who went to technical schools (schools soon to disappear) and the large majority, the 'ordinary metal children', who went off to a less academic curriculum in the local 'secondary modern' (Simon, 1991). As children in primary schools across the nation were streamed and groomed for the eleven-plus, anxious parents perpetually asked the question: why was it that a child's chances were to be decided at 11? Families became split and alienated as one or more of their children crossed the road to a superior school and a different set of life chances while the others disappeared into markedly inferior schools and jobs. The question of 'intelligence' arose and led to mass IQ testing, the results an apparently context-free measure of a child's potential. Historians have deconstructed this process, showing that IQ tests were unconsciously biased, unreliable and always subject to head teachers' final

A contemporary photograph of 1930's children playing as they swing on a lamp post. The intensity of children's play outside school and the meaningful learning through bodily activity was noted by many educators as a direct contrast to the passive docility in school caused by competitive examinations. Reproduced with permission of Popperfoto.com.

judgements about the suitability of the candidate for a more academic curriculum (Simon, 1991; Sutherland, 1984). The position of girls alone made any testing suspect as they constantly statistically outshone the boys. Results were deliberately weighted against them to maintain the number of boys going to grammar schools.

How did the teachers themselves experience this deep split in educational ideology? In the autumn of 1991 two elderly women, spinsters, both living alone in the same city but unknown to each other, related their life histories. Alice Hallouran, 83, and Alice Berridge, 87, had both been head teachers for over 30 years. Miss Hallouran had been head of a state infant school with over 400 children, Miss Berridge had been head of a boys' preparatory school. Now they are both dead, but their stories, told over several hours and returned to for confirming detail do, we believe, show some of the complex matrix of class, gender, power and choice that constructs teachers' values. And certain fragments of their testimonies begin to reveal how these values drive action and interpretation.

Miss Berridge

Miss Berridge was born in 1904, the fifth child in a family of six. Her father was Chief Constable of Barrow-in-Furness.

> I think I would be about 12 when we went to live in our own house in Abbey Road, which was a very nice district in Barrow. It was mostly what I would call a working class town. There were many lower class people, but I didn't really come across them. They were the poor children.

Miss Berridge was sent to train as a teacher at the Bedford Froebel College.

> It was 1922 and I was 18. My father went to see Miss Fordham, our headmistress to see if I could become a secretary. She said, No, the men were all coming back from the war and there wouldn't be any future for women secretarial. She suggested I went in for teaching. I wasn't consulted at all. And then she found out about Bedford, the Froebel College, where I went for three years.

> Without consulting me I was entered for Bedford Froebel College.

There were two National Froebel Colleges that offered training for the Froebel certificate, both of them private and essentially providing for upper middle-class girls.

> *There was Bedford and there was one at Roehampton. They were rivals those two colleges.*
>
> *There were certain big public schools – St Paul's School in London and Cheltenham Ladies College – Those schools – would always apply to Bedford when they wanted someone to teach ... They'd had people, and they always wanted the same sort of people. They relied very much on people who spoke well.*

Clearly matters of class and self-presentation were uppermost in Miss Berridge's mind. However the Froebel training was rigorous and wide-ranging.

> *It was an all round training. We did school subjects in our first year. Then in the second and third we did a lot of handwork. By the end of the summer term you had to produce things you made yourself. The idea was that children like using their hands, it was good for them to experience that sort of thing. Then in your third year you taught every day in the little practice school.*
>
> *You produced posters for children to see and apparatus for them to work with. It was like play to the children, in a way, but they were learning all the time. There were things like the 'Look and See' method when you had little cards, and they had musical games.*

Miss Berridge was so successful that on finishing her course she was asked to join the staff. But, strangely, despite this success, to her the whole Froebelian ideology was wrong:

> *I didn't feel I was giving my best and the students they didn't have enough drive. Very often I didn't think they drilled things into children as I wanted to – what I call the old-fashioned teaching which we're coming back to today. They did airy-fairy things ...*
>
> *I didn't like all the handwork they tried to do and they didn't do that successfully. They didn't get good results: the children made things that weren't worth having.*

Clearly the whole approach to child freedom made her uneasy. Children were empty vessels and needed to be trained.

I wanted the children to be taught as they had to be when I got to Manchester, as all the old boys will tell you who went there.

I would often step in and give a demonstration lesson and try to show them how to teach things to children, to really drive facts home.

At last in 1934 Miss Berridge found a job that was to suit her for the rest of her professional life. It was to head a new preparatory school for boys attached to a nineteenth-century grammar school in Manchester. Now she could settle with a teaching style that suited her philosophy:

Of course we always taught formally in the prep. They did a little handwork and they had games and gym, but we hadn't the facilities for projects or anything like that. They just had to sit in desks in rows.

Nevertheless the Manchester middle classes accepted and approved of her methods as the old-fashioned 'prep school' approach.

However, after the Butler Act of 1944 this comfortable arrangement was disturbed by the national desire for greater equality of opportunity.

When I first went before the War it was more or less automatic that the boys went to the main school. My top form was 10 year olds and they went on to a preparatory form in the school, because it was all fee-paying then. But then the 11 plus came in.

Opening the grammar schools to all children who had passed the eleven-plus meant her work became constricted in very particular ways. Paying fees at the preparatory phase was supposed to be preliminary to a free place at a top school. But it did not necessarily work. In her testimony again and again Miss Berridge referred to the pressure from parents and the grammar school itself leading to intensive teaching and coaching that went on around the eleven-plus examination in the private preparatory school.

We particularly trained them to take the 11 plus. The majority usually passed ... but there were always some who didn't pass. One year I had about eight who didn't pass the 11 plus and the headmaster of the grammar school came to ask me why.

For many years Miss Berridge ran the preparatory and worked away with the oldest class to get them through the eleven-plus.

> *I almost lost my soul through the 11 plus. I used to regard children when I interviewed them as to whether they could pass the 11 plus. You see, I'm very fond of children, I always have been, and I began to think I'm not seeing them as human beings, I'm assessing them ... But I don't think I would ever get rid of the 11 plus – not while there are grammar schools.*

Miss Berridge stayed head of the prep until she retired in 1969. The school continued to prosper. Indeed, the Manchester middle classes were often desperate to get their sons in to the preparatory – the only sure fire route to the prestigious grammar school. This was continually under pressure. Even when she went into hospital with appendicitis she remembers the surgeon attempting to persuade her.

> *He sat on my bed and said to the nurse, 'You may go now, nurse'. And he said to me, 'Miss Berridge I have a son who would like to come to the preparatory!' Would I consider having his son? I said as soon as I'd got a vacancy I'd let him know ...*

She lived through the war in Manchester and her flat was bombed and she had to move. As the years passed, the exigencies of getting children through the eleven-plus began to wear:

> *I didn't like the 11 plus for a long time. It changed my outlook – I found I was looking at children as possible candidates to get into a grammar school ... but it did make all teachers have certain standards if they hadn't them already.*

Miss Hallouran

Miss Hallouran was born in 1907 in Huddersfield. She was an only child. Her mother had left school at 11 to be a part-time worker in the nearby mill. Her father was a cabinet-maker.

> *My mother was a weaver. She worked part-time at the mill all her life until I earned a salary. I think she was a very intelligent woman but hadn't been given opportunities. She was a great reader and*

appreciated classical reading, although she didn't know they were classics. For example Tolstoy.

My father was a carpenter, rather a cabinet maker, and I think he was the kindest man, he never said a wrong word to anybody.

I was brought up in a back-to-back house. There aren't any left now. One room downstairs and two rooms up and an attic for drying the washing. The mill where my mother worked was nearby. You could hear the terrible clatter of the looms and the heat was dreadful.

As with Miss Berridge the social world began to sharpen and define itself in childhood. Inequalities of class became apparent and accepted:

My father's only sister married a man who worked in a bank. They had a biggish house and a car which was unusual in those days. So you see I moved about several times a year in different atmospheres.

There was, shall we say, a great deal of difference between the two households, my father's mother and that of my mother's family.

I went to school at five, of its type it was quite a good school – a Board school. It was in Huddersfield. We walked to school and we came back at dinnertime and went back in the afternoon. I remember being rather humiliated, I can still remember it, because my mother wore a shawl – it came over her shoulders – to take me to school, and women were going with hats on, but remember my mother worked in the mill. I had already begun to see at five years old that there was a difference between her and my paternal grandmother and those aunts who would never have dreamed of going out in a shawl.

In many cases children were denied the opportunity of secondary education and were expected to leave their elementary schools at 14.

There were a certain amount of free places for the very few and everybody else had to pay.

Anyway when we were 11 we took the scholarship exam. I had to write an essay on 'Hearts of Oak'! Then we had an interview if we passed the first part.

Of course you weren't allowed to go in for the exam unless they thought you had some idea ... about eight or so out of forty took the exam and about half of them passed ... about a tenth from my school. There were about a hundred people from the town who got into the High school ... I don't know how many children tried.

Miss Hallouran, like Miss Berridge, was not consulted about her future:

> *I remember my mother was sent for after I had finished the sixth form to see if I could go to University, I had passed the Cambridge Responsions you see, but my mother said no because she couldn't afford three years, she could only afford two.*
>
> *So I was only going to a training college, but I decided I could go to a London training college.*
>
> *The people at these higher training colleges were jolly good, because they would have all gone to university if they had had the money. We were the elite really, you see, because we were clever enough but we hadn't been able to afford to go to university. We nearly all turned out to be head teachers.*

After the two years at college Miss Hallouran had to find work:

> *The first people who came down were Liverpool and they offered me a place and I had to accept it. I didn't want to accept Liverpool, I wanted to stay in London, but I daren't disobey the Principal!*

In Liverpool Miss Hallouran started her probationary year. Probationers were not allowed to stay on in the school after that year and as a result could be exploited quite dramatically:

> *Well, I was put in a very, very large school in a huge new housing area. I was given a class of 50, and because I was the last comer and the school was overcrowded I had to have them in the hall. There were wooden dual desks, very heavy, and they were at the side of the hall. In the morning the whole school came in and had prayers. Immediately after prayers my 7-year-olds and myself moved 25 of these dual desks. We then proceeded to have some lessons and at play time we proceeded to move the desks back against the wall, and then we took our things into another classroom as other classes were coming in for their PT and so on.*
>
> *When the afternoon came we did it all again.*

Child health had become a major national anxiety after the First World War. Despite the obvious effects of poor nutrition most of the governing classes felt that fresh air was vitally important.

It was a new school with open-air principles. The windows came down to the floor and opened on each side and all the children's things blew out of the windows. It was 1929, which was a terribly bad winter, and the headmistress of the school refused to let us wear cardigans, so we had to wear overalls with cardigans underneath.

Under these harsh conditions, however, Miss Hallouran's reading and her belief in 'modern methods' began to grow and develop into a philosophy of pedagogy that was going to form her guiding principles for the rest of her professional life.

It was a bleak council estate. It had streets and streets and no trees, no grass, no anything.

I had read and believed in modern methods, and off we trotted one day to collect clay from where they were building and we came back with lumps of clay and the children each made pots from the clay.

It was terribly difficult to work with modern methods with 50 children under those conditions in the hall. I don't know that I was very successful but I tried.

The most important thing was that the Liverpool education people, the first year I went, had decided they were going to hold classes for the Froebel Certificate, but we had to pay for them.

The Liverpool Education Authority was encouraging probationary teachers to study the new methods and the philosophy behind them, so that we would be qualified Froebel teachers.

Miss Hallouran had very little money. Of the £12 she earned each week she sent home £4 to her parents.

I lived in digs and I paid 12 shillings for that and I lived mostly on egg and chips! I didn't have enough money to go out with the other young teachers so I scraped enough to do the Froebel Certificate.

It was really a very hard course. We went to the university for the history and education, we went to the art school for the art part, and we had to teach, and we took two years to do it. But it was the full course they would have taken if you'd been a Froebel student in a training college.

I went along to my Froebel classes and I did my bit trying to teach them with the clay pots and we did some weaving with little twigs with little bits of string. I tried to teach them according to what I was ... from the very start of my teaching career I was Froebel oriented.

When in 1928 Miss Hallouran consciously chose to be a Froebelian and to work with child-centred principles, despite the difficulties posed by the existing pedagogy and design of an ordinary elementary school, she was now aligning herself with the powerful alternative movement. As we have seen, the Hadow Report of 1931 clearly endorsed the Frobelian child-centred approach. Nevertheless it remained a great struggle to introduce new methods into existing schools.

> *It took two years of evening classes from 1928 to 1930 to gain the Froebel certificate. The head teacher in the school I was working in was not at all sympathetic. For the teaching part we had to do ten lessons and some Froebel inspectors would come and watch. But we only had to take 20 children for this and the headteacher insisted that I had to have the other 30 at the back of the class while I did the Froebel lesson!*
>
> *You see you tried to teach them according to their individual abilities and experiences, not as a class. It was rather dreadful considering the numbers ... I had 50 the first year.*

Undoubtedly it was the teacher training colleges that were responsible for the dissemination of Froebelian ideas in the early twentieth century, but the national Education Department was not far behind. Miss Hallouran remembered how the pupil teacher system of training had simply not allowed scope for the new approach.

> *An aunt of mine, who was an elementary teacher trained as a pupil teacher, said she had to go to classes at 7 o'clock in the morning with the head teacher of the school, and then she taught all day in the school. She took her certificate without any other training – simply an apprenticeship. And of course they didn't have time or inclination to bother with Method because they had the legacy of 'payment by results' in mind.*
>
> *Eventually I got a headship at Nelson in East Lancashire, it was near Burnley where I had an uncle.*

Miss Hallouran's appointment to headship in 1937 was part of the revolution of child-centred educational ideas that was spreading a new ideology of childhood across the country.

> *There I was appointed for a special reason, they wanted me to introduce the new methods, and I was told that by the Education Officer who was a perfect dear.*
>
> *It was a very formal school. In fact the children came in saluting a picture of the King, and it was King Edward who was dead for over twenty years – they hadn't even changed it! They had aspidistras in all the windows and a head teacher's desk at the top of the hall. I had to get rid of all those things.*
>
> *My aunt, who had been the pupil teacher, came into my bedroom one night and said 'You shouldn't have done that Allie'.*

New methods did not always 'take' when the basic approach had been so different for so long.

> *All the teachers were older than I was. They were very loyal really and willing to try things out. I made an activity room and each class spent a day in there, doing handwork and moving about freely. But I didn't really manage to get them to really change much of their methods inside their classrooms.*

Even in the infant school in the sight of the teachers was the great controlling axis of the 'scholarship' examination. These teachers worked hard at bringing quite young children up to the required standards in reading, writing and arithmetic, conscious of the fatigue and fear the children would suffer as the examination came closer, yet keenly controlled by their ambitions for their child pupils. Froebelians, who continuously attacked the system, discovered that even in infant schools there were extra classes for potential scholarship children. In the elementary schools they showed that many children were frightened, and that often the promotion of teachers depended on the number of scholarships gained in their school. As Miss Hallouran described:

> *The children went on to a senior elementary school and were trained up for the scholarship exam four years later. The scholarship lists were published in the local paper and all my infant teachers took a great interest in these lists. They had predicted which children would get them and worked towards that when they were only seven! By*

1937 the Inspectorate were advocating freer methods but things didn't change much at Nelson.

One teacher was young, about my age and she had been at training college. She told me the former head had told her to forget everything she had learnt at training college, 'You do what I say here' he had said.

Miss Hallouran was to move on after three years to her final headship in Cambridge. But the fragility of a child-centred vision in the face of authoritarian methods and hierarchies was made clear to her when she once returned to Nelson.

I met my friend, the younger teacher, in the street and she said to me 'Do you know what I've got in this suitcase? It's newspaper'. I had taught her that there are few things that children can really go hell for leather and make a real mess with, we are always telling them to be careful, and it was wartime. I had suggested to her that they could have as much newspaper as they liked and cut and cut and cut. They had got this new head who didn't believe in this sort of child freedom, so she'd still take her newspaper, but she didn't dare put it in the wastepaper basket!

I was head in Cambridge of the Sanditon School for thirty years. I believe I kept my Froebelian principles but I couldn't always get my staff to carry them into practice.

You see it all depends on the dedication of the teachers what is happening.

How do we make sense of these records of life's experience? It was Miss Berridge, tall daughter of a chief constable, who considered herself 'too fierce' to teach in the kindergarten, who turned away from her years of Froebelian training and 'taught formally' in her boys' preparatory school. Despite her years in the Froebel college itself, she found herself working with what she felt was the essential technology of the eleven-plus. Her social and educational duty became a long struggle to get as many middle-class boys, sons of the Manchester bourgeoisie, into a grammar school. Perhaps it was because here she had an opportunity to 'drill things into children', to secretly guess what would be on the examination papers and teach the boys accordingly, to make sure they covered all the work and 'jolly well knew their tables'. 'Airy fairy' teaching was not her way. The boys sat in rows and faced her at the front. Their parents had paid fees so that they would 'win' free places at the grammar school and she did not want to let them down. And yet she recognized that the technology of a pedagogy based on relations of explicit disciplinary power was in place – surveillance, normalization of individual difference through tests and standards, and overall the great axis of the hierarchical relations of power – the controlling examination of the eleven-plus. Thus childhood became developed for her, despite her Froebelian training to the contrary, as an instrumental preparation for adulthood, a time of dense preparation, of correction and obedience.

> I could only teach formally in the sort of building we had. We just had to sit in desks in rows, but I was quite happy to use those methods. But I am lucky, I always had children and parents who wanted them to suceed.

Her life in teaching children contrasts dramatically with Miss Hallouran's sense of the sanctity of childhood against a background of its denial:

> I believe each stage in life should be lived as well as you can in the present. I don't think you should be thinking of adulthood at all with children. They are people in themselves at the same time. The scholarship exam and the 11 plus was like an apprenticeship for a job rather than education.

In these fragments chosen from the dense narratives of experience that these women related, certain issues behind the social construction of the work of primary teachers and the choices they can make in classroom and staffroom stand out. Why did Miss Berridge and Miss Hallouran make the choices they did? The matrix of experience, particularly in childhood, the political assumptions of the family and class from which they sprang, the inner conviction that grows throughout their lives' struggles, the frameworks of interpretation that the discursive networks within which they made sense of the civic world around them were all fused into their sense of themselves and their mission. These women demonstrated a strong sense of agency in the world they inhabited, and made their choices with clear-sighted, rational opportunism and a strong sense of what was right. And yet they were ideological *opponents*. They took part in a war of ideas that raged around them about the nature of schooling for young children and lived their lives honourably committed to values which formed an ideological position on which they both had opportunities to renege.

FURTHER READING

Cunningham, P. (1988) *Curriculum Change in the Primary School Since 1945: Dissemination of the Progressive Ideal.* Lewes: Falmer Press.

Foucault, M. (1977) *Discipline and Punish: The Birth of the Prison.* London: Allen Lane.

Holmes, E. (1911) *What Is and What Might Be.* London: Constable and Co Ltd.

Lawrence, E. (ed.) (1952) *Friedrich Froebel and English Education.* London: Routledge and Kegan Paul.

Sutherland, G. (1984) *Ability, Merit and Measurement: Mental Testing 1880–1940.* Oxford: Oxford University Press.

Wollons, R. (ed.) (2000) *Kindergartens and Cultures: The Global Diffusion of an Idea.* New Haven, CT, and London: Yale University Press.

chapter 3

PLOWDEN AND BEYOND

CHILD-CENTRED TEACHING AND THE COMPREHENSIVE IDEAL

As we have seen, the race for grammar school places affected the whole education system. Although after the Second World War there was a widely held belief in a more liberal, creative and child-centred approach to the primary aged child, teachers, administrators and parents were caught in a system that rewarded measured 'academic' ability at an early age. Despite the child-centred ideals of the 1931 Hadow Report, primary schools could not be released from the straitjacket of training and grooming children for the eleven-plus. By the early 1960s, the vast majority of junior primary schools in England and Wales were organized in response to the demands of this crucial examination. Children were grouped according to their age and abilities, and teaching methods consisted of careful instruction in reading, writing and arithmetic, using highly structured, teacher-led approaches to learning. Here, as the historian Brian Simon has shown, the grading and grouping mirrored the class system, so that the children of manual workers were to be found in a large proportion in the lower streams, placed there from an early age and rarely moved upwards, while children of wealthier parents dominated the top streams (Simon, 1991: 345). The training colleges in most cases deplored this situation and many young teachers saw their child-centred ideals turn to dust in the teeth of this desperate competition for places at grammar schools. Creative educationalists, such as

Cambridgeshire's Sybil Marshall, showed the way a rural primary school could cater for all abilities and enhance the children's autonomy and independence through a creative curriculum, but it was to no avail while the eleven-plus held sway.

Many parents, too, loathed the system, despite the subsequent loud lament for the demise of grammar schools. It is important to remind ourselves how unpopular the selection process was with most parents, particularly those, including many middle-class families, who had, or risked having, their children at very different schools. At last, in 1965 the Labour government issued their famous Education Circular 10/65, which instructed local education authorities to draw up plans to move away from the existing selective forms of secondary schooling towards a more *comprehensive style* of organization and provision. Over the next ten years and more, county after county slowly submitted plans that switched their schools to the comprehensive system, abolishing their grammar schools and secondary moderns and replacing them all with co-educational comprehensives. It is easy to forget how popular this move was. Even the conservative Mrs Thatcher, no friend of the comprehensive ideal, coming to power as Minister for Education in the Heath government of 1970, oversaw the institution of over 2,000 comprehensives across the nation.

THE PLOWDEN REPORT: *CHILDREN AND THEIR PRIMARY SCHOOLS*

This massive change to secondary education in the late 1960s released primary education from its enchainment. In 1967 the government published one of the most remarkable reports on primary education ever configured, a lasting attempt by an industrialized democracy to enhance the creativity and autonomy of all its children, the Plowden Report. This official report of the government appointed committee, chaired by Lady Brigid Plowden, will be ever remembered for its almost extraordinary synthesis of values and practice in its recommendations for the education of English and Welsh 5–11-year-olds. Taking the same child-centred approach as the Hadow Report of 1931, this committee had a fresh chance to build a primary system that embraced not only pedagogy, but also to take into account the deprivation of children in poorer areas. In this it boldly incorporated current social research, producing a joined-up, anthropological document on primary education that was needed to fulfil its highest ideal, of producing a creative, autonomous, yet responsible and moral young citizenry across the nation.

The Plowden Report's child-centred principles were boldly articulated in its most famous passage: 'At the heart of the educational process lies the child. No advances in policy, no acquisitions of new equipment have their desired effect unless they are in harmony with the nature of the child, unless they are fundamentally acceptable to him' (Plowden Report, 1967, ch. 2: 9).

Recognizable by its intense focus on method, the Plowden Report called for an end to separate grouping of children by their measured abilities and levels of achievement in all primary schools. It placed renewed emphasis on more informal and flexible teaching techniques, recommending group working in primary classes through a project approach to teaching and learning. It positively encouraged far more art, drama, music, and creative and personal writing within a more seamless curriculum which should, it avowed, flow across the time blocks of the child's school day. The Report went on to cover pre-school education, the ages and stages of schooling and continuity between them, internal organization of schools and the roles of adults in schools, buildings, and promoting of ongoing research and innovation.

Clearly the Plowden Report set out to reform and modernize the entire system of primary schooling. Another famous passage set about reconceptualizing the whole relationship between teacher and young learner:

> A school is not merely a teaching shop, it must transmit values and attitudes. It is a community where children learn to live first and foremost as children and not as future adults. In family life children learn to live with people of all ages. The school sets out deliberately to devise the right environment for children, to allow them to be themselves and to develop in the way and to the pace appropriate to them. It tries to equalize opportunities and compensate for handicaps. It lays special stress on individual discovery, on first hand experience and on opportunities for creative work. It insists that knowledge does not fall into neatly separated compartments and that work and play are not opposite but complementary. (Plowden Report, 1967, Ch. 1: 187–8).

Famously, the Report also covered issues of the home, school and neighbourhood, introducing the notion of Educational Priority

Areas for certain areas with high levels of socio-economic deprivation. In essence, the effects of the Plowden Committee's recommendations were to demand a return to the child-centred and humanitarian approaches to primary schooling first set out in the 1931 Hadow Report. This time, without the constricting presence of selection for secondary school, the Plowden Report's recommendations were acknowledged and, in theory at least, slowly adopted and adapted by the great majority of the nation's primary schools.

THE IDEOLOGY OF PLOWDEN

There is no doubt that, underlying the eight volumes of detailed information and prescription that constitutes the Plowden Report is a distinct and reasonably coherent system of values. Indeed it was, for many years, regarded as an important document because of the large amount of educational theorizing it contains. It openly endorsed what it saw as the natural development of the growing child and demanded that all teaching in primary schools should be sensitive to each child's innate development. For this reason the curriculum should be open and thematic rather than closed and subject based. The time breaks and the organization of the school should favour the autonomy and independence of each child so that he or she should not be interrupted in their projects and learning. The teacher should not regularly instruct but be a guide and counsellor for each learning child, facilitating learning through providing resources, questioning and supporting rather than teaching in more direct or didactic ways.

Peters
Because of its explication of and dependence on theory, including the developmental psychology of Jean Piaget, the Plowden Report was soon treated as an authoritative text on primary education in colleges of education, and as such it soon acquired a number of qualifying critiques that students were expected to read alongside it. Perhaps the most famous of these was *Perspectives on Plowden* in 1969 edited by the philosopher Richard Peters. Peters and his co-authors did not set out to attack the recommendations of the Plowden Report for they believed that 'by and large they would, if carried out, lead to a marked improvement in primary school education'. They held that the Plowden Report 'represented a great advance on the more authoritarian thinking that came before it'. Nevertheless, as Peters put it, its summary of 'educational philosophy proliferates in important half truths'. They are as follows:

1 The child has a 'nature' which will 'develop' if the appropriate environment is provided.
2 Self-direction is very important in this development.
3 Knowledge cannot be divided into separate compartments.
4 The teacher must be a guide, an arranger of the environment rather than an instructor.

Peters deconstructs each of these ideas in an effort to achieve precision. What is 'development'? he asks, pointing out that, 'outside of a context this term is one of vacuous recommendation that is consistent with any form of development'. Why is self-direction more important that working with others? Here he argues that too little is known about the ways autonomy, independence and 'creativity' are developed. As for not compartmentalizing different subjects, surely, he asks, 'one of the great achievements of our civilization is gradually to have separated out and got clearer about the types of concepts and truth criteria involved in different forms of thought?' Finally, as to the role of the teacher, he believes the report 'systematically ignores the inescapably social character of thought and language, of transmission and of motivation' (Peters, 1969: 1–20).

Bernstein and Davies

In the *Perspectives* other distinguished philosophers such as Robert Dearden and sociologists such as Basil Bernstein also attempted to clear away much of the 'muddled thinking' in the Plowden Report. Bernstein and Brian Davies claim, for example, that much of the social data collected for Plowden was misinterpreted – particularly to endorse dubious theories of *cultural* deprivation. Several important factors, they argued, demonstrate more *structural* aspects of social and economic class, rather than individual family differences. All in all, *Perspectives on Plowden* remains an important corrective to some of the 'philosophical', and too much taken for granted, ideas in the report without fundamentally attacking its manifest liberal and inclusive approach to children expressed in its recommendations.

ATTACK FROM THE RIGHT: THE BLACK PAPERS

It was not long however before the Plowden Report's child-centred agenda was under furious attack from more conservative critics. In what seems in retrospect a rather muddled but intensely written set of pamphlets, collectively known as the Black Papers, several public intellectuals entered the educational realm (Cox and Dyson, 1971).

The late 1960s in Britain had seen student unrest spread from America across the western world and in this turbulent decade the old principles of the Enlightenment – that all structures of authority should be questioned by the young – were once again seen to have revolutionary consequences. A breakdown in order and respect for authority was washing through the universities, manifested by sit-ins and marches by students demanding more power and autonomy. In castigating what they saw as the 'liberal left' architects of this youthful irresponsibility, major academic commentators saw the new relaxed, even permissive, practices of primary education as directly implicated. Indeed 'progressive' education at all levels in the system was, they claimed, directly responsible for this anarchy and confusion. Most of the authors of these widely read pamphlets did not, however, wish to return to the eleven-plus and the cruelties of selection, but they called loudly for a return to discipline and subject taxonomies, examinations and the restoration of, to them, abandoned meritocratic academic systems in primary and secondary schools.

Forty years on the 'notorious' Black Papers still make interesting reading. Written by a miscellany of dons, schoolteachers, writers and journalists, the whole scene of British education was depicted as dangerously anarchic. First, they commented on student militancy, 'left wing student interference with traditional academic freedoms', as they put it. Second, they focused on the 'falsification of facts' that they claimed was used to justify Plowden's progressive turn. Third, they attacked the whole ideal of the comprehensive school – claiming it would be responsible for a decline in standards and a reduction in opportunities for able children. In these respects one of their most remarkable features is their extraordinary anxiety about *boys*. In fact girls – and their necessary education – are almost completely invisible in the whole collection. This is not simply a result of the contemporary use of the male pronoun, now abandoned in all public documents as gender has become a category within history and social science, but a genuine, single-eyed concentration on the young male. The main arguments swirl around the 'bright boy' and how he is to be identified and promoted through the system. Little did they realize how soon the girl child was to forge ahead of her brothers. Far more competent in the post-industrial labour market where flexibility and adaptation are the qualities needed, supported through feminist networks, increasingly present in elite professions and institutions, and continuing to out-shine her male counterparts at examinations, she now makes the Black Papers look dated and irrelevant. Whatever the progressive comprehensive system did or did not do for boys, the authors of the Black Papers did not imagine that the invisible girls, even many working-class girls, would soon relatively thrive within the reformed system of schooling.

ATTACKS FROM THE LEFT

What was far more devastating and poignant to the believers in child-centred education, because they often rightly see themselves as radical in their approach to children, was the Marxist attack on its pedagogy – the terrible blow from the Left. It was not long after Plowden and comprehensivization that various left-wing intellectuals saw in progressive child-centred education, not a breakdown in the law and order of the primary school, but a sinister move of the bourgeoisie to disguise power relations and social control through new forms of almost invisible coercion. Child-centred approaches became characterized by various sociologists, all influenced more or less strongly by Marxism, as a deliberate move away from *explicit* disciplinary practices which could be understood and eventually resisted by working-class children – such as shouting, beating, grading and examining – to implicit, difficult to grasp, *covert* forms of surveillance and direction – a sort of 'soft control' that continues to promote the class interests of the middle and upper classes within the very processes of classroom discipline.

In empirical terms these neo-Marxist scholars were undeniably accurate. Several key studies of pedagogy in infant and junior schools in the 1970s showed primary teachers imposing their own, usually very middle-class, mores on young children through *implicit* means (Sharp and Green, 1975). Instead of 'Be quiet' young children were now admonished through indirect references such as 'Somebody is talking'. In place of straight directives to bad behaviour such as 'You have needlessly spilt the paint', children were asked 'Won't Mummy be disappointed when she sees your jumper?' Indeed, the left-wing critique of Plowden became extended through ideas of discourse. The child-centred discourse of the report itself, which attempted to make the exigencies and brutalities of social class into an optimistic classless exercise in treating all children as the same, to Marxists simply normalized the experience and thus behaviours of the middle-class child and pathologized the different experiences and responses of the working-class child. By 'softening' the techniques of control and instigating 'false freedoms' in the curriculum the child-centred teacher simply becomes, they argued, an agent of a new but hidden form of class repression.

Much of this critique is unanswerable without new terms of reference. First, it must be stated repeatedly and strongly that child-centred teaching does not abdicate from explicit adult control over children. However, in moving to more indirect forms of discipline it tries to keep an ideal in place of a rational republic where children can grow and flourish as individuals and at the same time develop a sense of community. 'Somebody is talking' brings home to the child that he or she is a member of a school community that must function in certain ways. 'Won't Mummy be disappointed when she sees your jumper?' is a complex piece of discourse that calls up the autonomy of the independent child and how he or she is part of a web of mutually responsible beings within a family community. In the child-centred approach to control, implicit disciplinary techniques are used not just to govern but simultaneously to develop a sense of justice and responsibility. To claim that this is a slide to implicit from explicit forms of discipline is not entirely wrong, but the critique is too reductively focused on techniques of control, losing the overtones of the complex nature of the teaching and learning relationship that can flourish within the child-centred ideal. Second, in these accounts there is something lacking in the interpretation of evidence. In one of the most famous attacks on child-centred ideology, *Education and Social Control* by Rachel Sharp and Anthony Green (1975), the empirical evidence for child-centred ideology working primarily as a form of social control is very loosely garnered and somewhat clumsily interpreted.

THE FEMINIST CRITIQUE

One important and resounding area of critique of child-centredness which grew alongside these Marxist accounts, and was partially influenced by them, was from those feminist scholars who focused on the woman primary teacher. To feminists of this sort, the kinds of suffering woman teachers (the gender of most of the primary teaching force) experienced within a school devoted to child-centred rhetoric were complex but severe. Made responsible for the orderly progress of the young children in her care, child-centredness meant that the woman teacher was simultaneously denied the very means of explicit disciplinary authority that would enable her to keep order. Now banned from shouting or ordering children to be quiet, from simply instructing them in a time-honoured act of teacherly transmission, from setting them in visible ability groups, or from offering them explicit punishments and rewards for their behaviour, the teacher becomes, they argued, in various ways a victim of fashionable ideology. In the most famous of these accounts, the child-centred primary teacher, usually a woman, is expected to carry the burden of society's demands and guilt with regard to their children without any of the support, authority, or disciplinary wherewithal to allow her to do the job easily and effectively (Steedman, 1985). Again a range of sociologists have pointed out that in dealing with working-class children there often exists a cleft between the soft control demanded by child-centred approaches and the real economically deprived circumstances of many 'differently', that is, 'badly behaved', children who are used to and expect more explicit disciplinary rules. Children whose parents do not share the middle-class values and behaviours of their teachers are often characterized as 'difficult' by the would-be child-centred teacher. As these scholars point out, this can be construed as a direct and unfair attack by middle-class observers, in the tradition of nineteenth-century charity women, on working-class child-rearing practices, that show no awareness of the true exigencies of poverty.

THIRTY YEARS AFTER PLOWDEN

From the return of the Conservative government in 1987 under Mrs Thatcher there was a steady erosion of child-centred ideology in primary schools. Bit by bit, under continuous attack from the Conservative Front Bench and particularly from a series of education ministers, the English primary school was returned to a more authoritarian elementary school ideology. In 1988 a whole new Education Reform Act introduced a National Curriculum with a series of published 'attainment targets'. This was the beginning of new formalized knowledge for primary aged children and a new ladder of targets to be 'driven up' in a newly imposed subject taxonomy. Time slots for separate subjects were reintroduced and Plowden's 'project method' was heavily disparaged. Mixed ability teaching, with children given a certain amount of independence over their work and tasks, was inexorably replaced with ability groups and timetables, groups whose performance could be measured against the new targets.

Throughout the 1990s across the industrialized world child-centred ideology was in retreat as in Europe and America national governments bowed under market pressure to measure, compare and improve – that is, formalize – their education systems. It was felt by many politicians that educational success, measured by tests for different age groups, meant economic success, although the causal link has never been proven and is more likely to work the other way round. As teaching for the test became daily practice in many English primary schools, the emergence of the 'tiger' economies in south-east Asia seemed to show that high results in formal skills tests, such as basic spelling and arithmetic, were key factors in economic growth. The subsequent collapse of those economies has since shown those nations the importance of liberal values and institutions, and several of them are now, ironically for Britain, seeking to liberalize their education systems. On the one hand, in Japan, where the economic stasis has endured for the longest time, there has been a drift to the Right, and, recently, reform of the basic law of education in quite reactionary ways. In China, Singapore, South Korea and Taiwan, on the other hand, ways of allowing independence of mind and creativity in the young are being sought out by educators and politicians as better markers of future economic success.

THE RECENT TEN YEARS

Nevertheless, after coming to government in 1997 the New Labour party set their policies behind the idea that economic success depended on tight central control of education with training and the invention of education attainment targets for all ages and stages. The outgoing Conservative government had reintroduced the testing of children. Regular annual tests for 7-, 14- and 16-year-olds were instated. Interestingly, with the memories of the old eleven-plus still affecting many parents, there was a time gap before the tests of 11-year-olds were introduced. But inexorably, in 1997, they came. The New Labour government in fact kept the whole Conservative education structure in place. Deeply believing its own rhetoric, the Blair government introduced a further plethora of 'reforms' based on measurement of targets and 'performativity'. In addition, the new government kept the Conservatives' policy of 'naming and shaming' what they characterized as 'failing schools'. That two-thirds of these were schools attended by poor, ethnic minority and special needs children not wanted by other schools was finally accepted, and the completely ineffectual public humiliation of schools and teachers was abandoned in late 1998 (Tomlinson, 2001: 90).

However, a whole raft of policies continued to be introduced to ensure ever tighter control by central government over the curriculum and the monitoring of standards. The role of the central inspection body, the Office for Standards in Education (Ofsted), was strengthened to include a range of disciplinary powers over schools, which soon impacted directly on the careers of individual teachers and head teachers. There was certainly a considerable rise in anxiety among teachers as they now struggled with the performance of children in their care in tests and targets. Indeed, New Labour policy deliberately set out to police teachers' work, with management of their performance based on private sector models, using parents as vigilantes in scanning league tables and helping in classrooms. Individuals and bodies appointed by central government, were set up to control major education decision-making and spending. Despite a rhetoric of social inclusion, the whole thrust of policy was to distinguish between children in ways that meant that classrooms soon became organized according to sets and ability groups, a practice that soon affected peer-based creative work and social relationships.

The rise of enormous numbers of training schemes and new qualifications, of curriculum edicts and materials, and the establishment of new quasi-government organizations in education, have not had much effect on most parts of the British economy. As Sally Tomlinson points out, economic successes in the past 20 years have come about primarily through financial and capital movement, especially since the major financial deregulation measures of the mid-1980s (Tomlinson, 2001: 156). Indeed, the narrowing of education to economic ends has not proved effective in raising economic performance, while having a detrimental effect on education's potential for liberalizing and humanizing the development of a young child's personality. Nor have standards risen. Despite a series of mendacious government claims to the contrary, a perpetual series of adjustments to the ways children, teachers and schools are measured, and considerable teaching to the test, there is little valid evidence that standards in English, Mathematics and Science have genuinely risen in primary schools since 1997 (Hilton, 2007; Tymms, 2004).

What has risen dramatically in that period are the ever-increasing numbers of disciplinary exclusions and voluntary truancies from English primary schools. Although the New Labour government seems to be trying to establish elements of inclusionary practices, it retains faith in market competition and fails to acknowledge some of the fundamental problems with a market-driven system in schools and local authorities. As we have seen in Chapter 2, with our long view of the eleven-plus and selection for secondary school, the intense focus on standards and assessment of children means the introduction of ever more narrow mechanistic targets that force schools to be more concerned with achievement (narrowly defined) and less receptive to challenging or difficult pupils. Miss Berridge's heartfelt cry 'I wasn't seeing them as children any more' reminds us of the dehumanizing effects of tests and measurement. As Fielding has pointed out, such a competitive framework also strips out the important elements of political debate and elevates clarity of measurement over any meaningful discussion of the right philosophy of education for young people in schools (Fielding, 1999). History shows us that a renewed child-centred philosophy can only be put in place when all young children are removed from the centre of a competitive assessment framework. In our next three chapters we argue for the enduring philosophical principles on which a revived child-centred tradition must be constructed in the twenty-first century.

FURTHER READING

Perhaps the most important and comprehensive work of history of education in this period is:

Simon, B. (1991) *Education and the Social Order*. London: Lawrence and Wishart.

The Plowden Report (1967) can be downloaded from: www.dg.dial.pipex.com/documents/plowden.shtml

Fielding, M. (1999) 'Target setting, policy pathology and student perspectives: learning to labour in new times', *Cambridge Journal of Education*, 29 (2): 277–89.

Fielding, M. (2000) 'Community, philosophy & education policy: against the immiseration of contemporary schooling', *Journal of Education Policy* 15 (4): 397–415.

Fitz, J., Davies, B., and Evans, J. (2006) *Educational Policy and Social Reproduction: Class Inscription and Symbolic Control*, London: Routledge.

Steedman, C. (1985) '"The Mother Made Conscious": the historical development of a primary school pedagogy', *History Workshop Journal*, 20: 149–63.

Tomlinson, S. (2001) *Education in a Post-welfare Society*. Buckingham: Open University Press.

part II

FUNDAMENTAL VALUES

chapter 4

THE 'WHOLE CHILD' AS A PERSON

In this next section we consider the philosophical principles and values on which a renewed version of child-centred education could be constructed for the twenty-first century. Clearly our historical child-centred legacy is rich with ideas and starting points. In opposition to the idea that childhood is simply a time of preparation for adulthood, we have the old conviction, insisted upon in Locke, Rousseau and the Froebelian kindergarten philosophy, that childhood is a *time in itself* and that the grown adult can only be secure and act authentically if during that period of early childhood, the child is allowed space, opportunity and time to develop his or her own pattern of consciousness. During this time of childhood, the historical child-centred tradition insists that the child's body and mind should be allowed considerable freedom, for it is only through the 'instinct to play' that the child comes to know and understand the world in its fullness and fascination. Indeed, the old idea of sense impressions still opens an important space for educators, for within this tradition the child's most early experiences are seen to be of vital importance to his or her pattern of development. Here, since Locke, the drives of curiosity and natural desire feature within the idea of authentic learning. Playing, experimenting children come to new knowledge in sensual, affective and active ways that enable them to understand its substance. In making new understandings and gaining knowledge in this way, children are seen to create knowledge for themselves rather than absorb and replicate it. It is in this sense that the child-centred tradition can be viewed as creative.

Within this creative tradition, handed down to us through history, there lies a deep and continuing respect, not for precocious performance or verbal fluency, but a strong feeling of the complex ways that consciousness of the material and social world is slowly developed, so that the child's inner life, his or her subjectivity, is treated with respect and sympathy – demanding a necessary following, as the Edgeworths put it, of children's 'zigzag' trails of thought and understanding. Finally, history has bequeathed us in this tradition alternative ways of teaching that are more democratic and mutually respectful between teacher and young learner than the authoritarian pedagogy of transmission teaching. Within the child-centred tradition the nourishing of the child's life through education by older members of their culture can only take place through and within practices of shared and sympathetic exchange.

How then do we go about constructing a contemporary, twenty-first-century conceptualization of child-centredness – of the ways all children could and should be at the centre of their own education? Here a much used phrase 'the whole child' is crucial to our argument. Often used in educational parlance, but rarely elaborated, the idea of the 'whole child' is sometimes merely an aphorism or cliché and needs to be unpacked if we are to try to find out what this can, or should, mean as an educational idea. We will start by examining what counts as the 'whole child', offering a version that includes an emphasis on personal authenticity, meaningful understanding and the importance of children being able to develop a strong sense of themselves through their education. A clearer view of what is entailed when we speak of the 'whole child' will allow us eventually to discuss what the implications of this view might be for educational practice.

To begin to clarify the idea, we need to set this 'holistic' notion of the child against the alternative, more reductionist view of childhood that has prevailed within, and indeed influenced, educational provision for many years. This latter view is based on the old assumption that childhood should be viewed basically as a preparation for future adulthood. Many decisions about the nature of education have been made with this emphasis on what is predicted or imagined is needed for the future, and this has allowed a range of ideas to become accepted as 'good' education. As examples, competition and assessment are often both justified in part as 'good preparation for the realities of adult life', workplace experience is now built into the curriculum for older children and even primary education has seen its share of 'entre-preneurial' activity increased in the name of the future interests of the economy. Now some of these arguments may have credibility, and others even seem to stress the importance of real experience, but for child-centred educationalists the importance of determining both rich and real experiences for children, *without* looking in such explicit terms to the future, has always been more important.

One argument against directing education by aiming for a desired future state would be that it is actually quite problematic to predict in any specific sense, what will be needed in the future, either for society or for individuals. To base education on those ideas alone is therefore misguided. In addition, by standing against those who stress society's future needs and what is advocated to be in a child's future interest, child-centred educationalists would claim that rich educational experience in the *present* should be our main concern. While considerations for the future should not be neglected, rich educational experiences are essential because these promote enjoyment in learning which helps to create open, interested persons who enjoy engaging with the world – persons who are committed to developing their understanding in whatever human context they might eventually find themselves. Rich educational experiences then are the best preparation of all for lifelong learning and the future as a whole. The next demand has to be to specify what might count as 'rich educational experience', but the shorthand often used for looking more broadly than the child as future economic capital, is to claim that education should be of the 'whole child', so it is to explicit consideration of what this could mean that we need to turn initially.

Child-centred education is often used to explain that the key idea involved is the notion that the child, in her or his entirety, should be the main consideration at the heart of what we determine education to be. It is therefore, as we said earlier, a claim that questions what exactly is meant by the idea of the 'whole child'? Now while the idea of education attending to the 'whole child' may appear to gather general support from many different perspectives on education, one assumption that needs to be challenged initially is that the idea of the 'whole child' just means a school system that simply works, usually at different times of the day, to develop both mind *and* body. In other words, all we need to show a concern for the 'whole child' is a standard kind of schooling that attends to the physical side of a child where exercise and what might count as healthy living is thrown in alongside the 'real' education that focuses on the intellect. Currently, there are important moves to stress that we need to educate both the body and the mind, and nutrition and health lobbyists have had some valuable influence in broadening the curriculum and even revising the aims of the curriculum. However, as we shall try to explain, for child-centred practitioners and theorists, a richer, more integrated notion of mind, body and personhood lies at the heart of the idea of the 'whole child'. And the first point to make is to highlight the word 'integrated', for many believe western thought, and thus educational practice, has suffered from false dualisms in our thinking of what it is to be human that seem to split mind from body and that go back centuries to Descartes and beyond. We have seen that there have been different perspectives over time in terms of what constitutes a person, in fact different perspectives about who would even count as having the potential to become a person. In current thinking, even if we could distinguish and then agree about what constitutes the mind and the body, and therefore how to feed or nourish each through education, what we decide to pack into the umbrella notion of personhood will be significant and can be different when viewed from alternative perspectives. Chapter 2 gave an account of two contrasting views from teachers and this chapter will begin by briefly examining two influential views on personhood that could be said to be reflected in those two teachers' beliefs. The chapter will go on to argue for the adoption of one view of a person rather than the other, and therefore suggest that to claim to educate the 'whole child', should be considered in the light of what it is to be a 'person'.

IS EDUCATION FIRST AND FOREMOST ABOUT THE DEVELOPMENT OF THE MIND?

We need to begin by asking what is involved in the very idea of a person. One fairly long-standing conceptualization of what it is to be a person that still has wide currency, and that we can perhaps see implicitly and to differing degrees in the views of both Miss Berridge and Miss Hallouran, is that consciousness, linked with a distinct physical body and point of view, ultimately constitutes a person as someone who can value things and make decisions and choices. Everyone is an individual but an individual only becomes a *person* in as much as she or he is capable of determining their own destiny and can represent 'an assertive point of view' (Peters, 1966: 211). We might say then that an individual becomes a person when they can think in particular ways and, above all, think for themselves. Out of this view would grow an educational emphasis on the capacity to make decisions and choices and, perhaps above all, use reasoning well. In current educational parlance this is a very powerful view that takes us squarely into the realms of advocating 'critical thinking' as the main mark of personhood (Bailin and Seigel, 2003). For many advocates, the idea of critical thinking is seen as the main means for achieving a central, if not *the* central aim of education – that of creating autonomous persons. Now the distinction between our two teachers might come not with this central aim but with regard to how this might be best achieved. For Miss Berridge, the emphasis might be on instructing children to teach them information and established knowledge, for only then will they be able to think and act for themselves. For Miss Hallouran, autonomy might be best achieved through the practice of allowing children some real independence and choice *as* they experience their lessons.

Let us visualize a discussion amongst children to see how this might work in practice. With sensitive but minimal support from their teacher, a group of 6-year-olds are discussing what they think might be entailed in the very process of thinking. One child asserts 'If you didn't have a brain, you wouldn't be able to think at all!' When questioned, he explains that we need our brains; they help us to stand up and think and speak. Across the circle, another child disagrees and claims that it is not with our brains, but we think with our hearts. Yet another claims that thoughts are quantifiable because 'At the end of the day I sometimes feel that I have used up all my thoughts'. Questioning, disagreement and lively exchanges, claims and counter-claims take the discussion forward with encouragement and some minor intervention from the teacher. In this captured episode of practice we can see that the powers of critical thinking are already present and there is also a clear capacity for these powers to be developed by the teacher. While Miss Berridge might find this exchange uncomfortable, too undirected and even pointless, her mission after the event would be clear, the need to correct misunderstandings would be paramount and possibly a single lesson could be devised to inform the children of the correct view of how we think. Even a less formally didactic teacher may also feel the need to move the children forward in their understanding to a more accepted view of thinking and this could be done by gentle questioning of the more naive statements to provoke further thinking, encouragement for those that lean towards an accurate conception of mind and, ultimately, the correction of any misunderstandings or wrong perceptions. For these kinds of teachers the process assumes that as these children pass through their education they should be encouraged to take a stance towards the world that allows information, problems and experience to be thoroughly probed in order to establish sound beliefs, decisions and judgements.

So here is a situation which, in different ways, might offer acceptable features of education for many teachers, even for some who would claim to be child-centred. One could argue that this could be part of a plausible account for what it means to have the child or person at the centre of their own education, because it highlights the idea that to educate a child is to help them become independent thinkers or more autonomous. Rational or personal autonomy as the central aim of education has an extensive following and, even when it is not explicitly advocated, it is implicit in much of the educational practice, and theorizing about practice, that has taken place throughout the past 50 years. However, for true child-centredness, we first have to ask if this gives us a sufficiently rounded view of the whole child, or is it a view that still skews the sense of a person, giving undue priority to intellectual development?

RICH 'EMBODIED' EXPERIENCE – THE WHOLE CHILD

Human beings come into existence as live, physical, sensing entities that, with support, can gradually mature and acquire a whole range of attributes beyond their intellectual development that make them persons. High on a list of the attributes for someone to 'qualify' as a person might well be consciousness and intentionality, or other features traditionally associated with the mind, but some would argue that there needs to be a continuing case for acknowledging the place of emotion, the senses and the physical side of life. Some mainstream philosophers are worth visiting here because they would endorse this view and go even further by suggesting that both our emotions and physicality should be considered as central within a truly comprehensive view of the mind. As we shall see, they point out that because the mind does not function without the body and feelings, these dimensions must be taken into account, thus in education we have to recognize that we are educating children and not just minds and we are educating in order for children to not just think in certain ways, but also to *act* in particular ways. We need a better story to explain how all these human characteristics interrelate and therefore direct us in ways that humans as *persons* should develop through education.

Welton   The philosophical idea that might support an enriched notion of the whole child begins with an argument for a more body-centred view of a person. This stems from the notion that while our minds are active in any experience we have of the world, it is a mistake to think of the mind as simply an inner function of the body. Instead, we need to acknowledge that we are first and foremost *embodied*, and furthermore that mind pervades our corporeal existence. Feelings and physicality are not separate, somehow sitting alongside our capacity to think, but integral with thought. A corporeal way of relating to the world can be seen, not just as important, but as *fundamental* to both being in and understanding the world. Some thinkers, for example, have famously argued that all current knowledge of the world, even scientific knowledge, is in essence gained from direct experience of the world without which the objective symbols we come to see as science would be meaningless. The philosopher Donn Welton expresses something of the contrast this gives with our standard account of approaching the world. He suggests that all objects are to be understood as *lived* objects long before they become objects for critical thought. He explains that, for example, scientific characterization can only grow from such things as:

> the ringing surfaces of the cobblestones on which I walk, with the rough board I am planing, with the supple face I embrace and hold in my hands. Surfaces that support, boards that are planed, faces that are embraced; they have an 'aesthetic' extension and then a flesh, one that our perceptions enfold, that is not yet the result of a categorical synthesis, of an act of cognition or, better, interpretation. (Welton, 1999: 53)

Now these ideas move us away from an exclusive emphasis on a particular kind of thinking, a dependence purely on the mind, that hitherto has determined the person. Subjectivity, emotion and even intuition enlarge the idea of what it is to be a person, and we begin to have a live sense of the extent to which experience influences who we become. However, to understand the full significance of the role of experience this very idea needs a closer look. Ultimately, educationalists must be interested specifically in educational 'experiences', but we need a full understanding of the general nature of experience before we can begin to distinguish what might be educational. In a general sense it is worth pointing out that all lived experience, what some have called our 'life-world', is concretely real and initially pre-theoretical, but from the beginning, because we are socially embedded from babyhood, our experiences and understandings are socially constructed. For example, the simple recognition of a teacup placed on a table is instantly augmented by an awareness that there are other perspectives that we cannot, at that time, physically see. Previous concrete experiences allow us, almost unconsciously, both to complete the full roundness of the cup and to understand its function, and these simple concrete experiences will have been continually informed by how others have seen and used the cup before we have even grasped for it. The process of how we consolidate our personal experiences into familiar and shareable patterns has important implications for education.

Merleau-Ponty

Merleau-Ponty is one philosopher who stresses the importance of the body to personhood. He explains that we need to pay closer attention to the bodily sensing and perception that accompanies our experience of being in the world, arguing that it is actually the body, not the mind, that is the true organ of experience (Merleau-Ponty, 1996). The body provides not just the first way of sensual engagement with the world but this physical experience retains its importance so that the sentient and sensuous body must be at the heart of even our most abstract thinking. Now this idea at first glance may seem either obvious or even trivial. However, because it relates well to the thinking in child-centred tradition, which stresses the value of concrete 'real' experience, it may be worth trying to understand the subtle distinctions that he is trying to draw our attention to. In his view, the body gives us a direction or perspective from which to relate to all things. Instead of a mere spectator or distant stance that attempts to analyse what happens in front of us, we need to realize that our bodies merge us into the very midst of things, and the things we perceive merge into us to give us the 'understanding' structures that help us make sense of our experiences. As in the example of the teacup, we cannot make sense from experience without perceiving and acknowledging that objects are bound up with the world and these basic structures for understanding the world become internalized within us. This means that human encounters with objects and others, should be seen as a form of dynamic, sensual and reciprocal activity that therefore requires openness and creative participation – we are continually engaged in an active and constant interplay between ourselves and the world. The implication for this in terms of education is that it is not only the extent and quality of children's concrete experiences that we need to look at, but the attitudes and dispositions that can be developed in order for children to make the fullest use and sense from those experiences.

These mainstream writers and philosophers are not writing specifically about education, but they are trying to articulate aspects of what it is to be a person and are challenging age-old assumptions that have in turn informed long-standing authoritarian views of education. The importance of their work to a child-centred view in education is that they offer an account of what it is to be a *fully experiencing* person who, importantly, can develop *in understanding*. It is a relatively easy step to see that this sense of a 'whole person' captures the old intuitive view that many child-centred teachers and educationalists have recognized and still want to embrace as a fundamental view of the child that should underlie educational practice. As the Edgeworths declared over 200 years ago, 'in this pernicious love of play he will discern the symptoms of a love of science, and, instead of deploring the natural idleness of children, he will admire the activity which they display in the pursuit of knowledge' (Edgeworth and Edgeworth, 1798: 30). We can link this with the earlier distinction made about looking to the present rather than the future and see that these ideas would be undoubtedly attractive, particularly to those who might enjoy spending time with children. As Miss Hallouran put it, 'I believe each stage in life should be lived as well as you can in the present. I don't think you should be thinking of adulthood at all with children. They are people in themselves at the same time'. But a rich set of experiences, with both children and teachers, contained in the pleasure of the present may hardly be enough to even count as education. Where does this take us in specific terms? If we do not look to the future adult, how can either teachers or learners derive a sense of purpose or direction to move learners forward from such a state of 'experiencing'?

PERSONAL DIRECTIVES

Cooper

One possible dynamic that is useful here comes from the ideas of existentialist philosophers being what the philosopher David Cooper calls a sense of 'directives'. His argument stems from the notion that

Embodied activity: playing to learn about ourselves

at any age, our very existence is, in effect, always an 'issue' for us. That issue is the struggle we have to engage in to make sense of what happens to us and to others in life. If we include some of the ideas we have already discussed, we have a notion of ourselves as both embodied and embedded in our own life-world, encountering experiences and ideas. To make sense of all this we need to interpret events and happenings. Some interpretations may be straightforward but others such as a personal loss or an exciting discovery may challenge our beliefs and the things that we care about. While we may see or learn how these ideas are received by others, it is our own authentic feelings and experiences that will count in the extent to which we can understand or make sense of these ideas. So, Cooper is suggesting that in the process of continually confronting the fundamental issue of the sense and meaning of our existence, we find ourselves trying to interpret our experiences and building some kind of picture or story of our life. As part of proceeding through life, we make decisions and choices and usually strive to do so in ways that seem wise and meaningful, guided by our beliefs and concerns. Cooper explains that these constituents should not be seen as features of character, but as something deeper and more binding because they are the means by which aspects of the world and our living have *meaning* and come to matter to us (Cooper, 1990: 14). It is these, the personal beliefs, concerns, values and interpretations that Cooper calls 'directives' that are significant, because ultimately they are what direct the very shape of a person's life.

Child-centred approaches could be said to draw on this insight with the idea of basing the curriculum on a child's interests. However, if the deeper notion outlined by Cooper is adopted, it is clear that the idea of 'interest' would have a very specific interpretation. Interests as whims and spontaneous preferences would not be seen as sufficiently weighty to constitute the substance of what is learnt. Instead, teachers would look to the deeper concerns of children for guidance, allowing the children's learning to focus on what the children themselves signal as significant and relevant to their current view of the world. One objection to this suggestion might be that concerns can overwhelm us and make us anxious at any stage in life. Are we really advocating that children should be concentrating on their concerns or could this lead to negative obsessing about the dangers and fears that are prevalent in our modern world? One response to make to this is that it is clear that children *do* have fears, both real and imagined, and for education to ignore these would be to renege on the basic commitment to educate. Some fears can be explained away with understanding, or tempered through empowerment. We might be prompted to change the way we act in the world by the fears we might have from seeing the fragility of the world in the face of global warming, for instance. Yet other fears can be faced and addressed through the safety of fictional contexts such as in fairy tales. Whatever way, the point is that children's concerns in this sense of fears are those areas that will need understanding and addressing in order to help them face and cope with life. These are therefore precisely the areas that education can, and arguably should, address.

Directives are, of course, much broader than just fearful concerns and so another question that could be raised is that while this notion of directives may be relevant to adults, how appropriate is it for young children? Do children conduct their lives through concerns, beliefs and values? One answer is that if education is to genuinely influence and touch the lives of children, it needs to at least begin with acknowledging the possibility and potential that children have for caring and belief. If we return to the classroom of 6-year-olds, we imagined the natural orientation for a teacher wedded to the centrality of prescribed adult knowledge would mean that her overriding aim might be to help the children come to a correct view of what thinking is. The one child's endearing comment that 'We think with our hearts' would, then, have to be replaced through scientific understanding by more accurate knowledge, and to pursue this directly would be seen as a mark of the respect that teacher had for the child. Here, alternatively, a teacher influenced by a commitment to the value of a child's authentic 'directives' might look from a different perspective and hold a completely different aim in mind. The 'correct' view about the function of the heart would be of less immediate importance than an acknowledgement of the strength and source of this child's present belief because we believe it to be expressed with great conviction. This is because, in turn, we hold that it is derived from her personal experience of the world. To take these beliefs seriously, and to allow the child to articulate and explore them further, would be to signal that the child's ideas matter and that school is an appropriate place to express genuine thoughts and concerns rather than a place just to learn the facts and adopt 'given/correct/adult' views. The gradual encouragement to express and respect one's own and others' authentic beliefs and concerns, it is suggested, actually helps to cultivate 'directives', and is a fundamental requirement for strengthening both independence and the capacity to flourish within life.

In this chapter we have argued that in order to understand and to revive some of the essential values embedded in child-centred education we need to begin by being clear what can be meant when someone claims that education should attend to the 'whole child'. The different ideas that have been discussed have led us to the point where we can suggest that educating 'persons' within a fresh child-centred view depends on seeing people as both embodied and embedded in the world. This view may be most recognizable when we consider how very young children experience their world, but it is important to stress that philosophically the analysis relates to all persons – and this then extends the idea beyond a particular age phase, to all children and, indeed, adults as well.

To summarize, the claim is that by focusing on the whole child in the senses discussed suggests that we should be constructing an education where, for example:

• senses and perceptions would be cherished and strengthened through experience
• beliefs would be taken seriously and explored
• expression of genuine concerns, things that matter, would be encouraged.

Memorable experiences: toasting marshmallows after a hard day of learning together in the forest

Some old key ideas associated with child-centredness have thus crept into this discussion to be reappraised. The value of child experience, expression and agency are implied but also qualified by what has been suggested so far. On the view and set of values we have mapped out, child-centred education calls for very particular kinds of learning experiences that offer the richness and primacy of sense, perception and recognition of the embodied mind. Furthermore, teachers would aim to inculcate in children an ability to savour and consciously to conceptualize their feelings and experiences without the rush to categorize and analyse along the lines of preordained knowledge frames. Each child's unique capacity for thought and agency would be valued so that teachers might encourage the expression of personal concerns and ideas. Learning would be steered in ways that allowed children to explore and strengthen their capacity for expression. The wealth of human 'established' knowledge need not be ignored, but instead could be seen as a resource – drawn upon as needed with support and guidance from a teacher. Some of these ideas will be fleshed out in Chapter 7 but, to summarize, schools operating with this central value of concern for the whole child would ensure that the educational experiences on offer for children would reflect the richness and primacy of sense, perception and embodied mind, for these are the fundamental means by which we can fully educate children.

FURTHER READING

Bonnett, M. (1994) *Children's Thinking*. London: Cassell.

Cooper, D. (1990) *Existentialism: A Reconstruction*. Oxford: Blackwell.

Darling, J. (1994) *Child-Centred Education and its Critics*. London: Paul Chapman Publishing.

Merleau-Ponty, M. (1996) Preface to 'Phenomenology of perception', in R. Kearney and M. Rainwater (eds), *The Continental Philosophy Reader*. London: Routledge.

Silcock, P. (1999) *New Progressivism*. London: Falmer Press.

chapter 5

MAKING SENSE: THE IMPORTANCE OF MEANING AND COHERENCE

In the previous chapter we approached the central child-centred notions of 'interest' and 'experience' through the idea that to respect a child's personhood means acknowledging that every child is an embodied mind, necessarily embedded in a primarily sense-based world. We began to explore beyond the idea that fleeting interest and mere bodily experience are enough for education and introduced the idea of 'directives' whereby humans are propelled through their lives by their values and beliefs, their personal projects and the things that really matter to them. The argument for education from a child-centred viewpoint is that these 'directives' are important considerations within education as well as life.

DETACHMENT VERSUS INVOLVEMENT

Heidegger It is worth reminding ourselves that these ideas are a fundamental challenge to the more standard view that humans have to gain understanding and knowledge of the world through disinterested study. On such a view, states of affairs, other people, and even ourselves are viewed as independent of anyone's individual experience of them. Indeed, personal experience is seen as faulty in some sense, or at least dangerous, because it risks being *merely subjective* and the main thrust of education is to move away from the child's personal, individual views towards the aspiration of collective, adult objectivity. This standard view goes on to suggest that education should therefore consist in helping children to analyse and objectify their idiosyncratic experience, thus helping them to learn to think critically about the world and ultimately endow them with accepted knowledge of how the world is constituted. One philosopher who, like others mentioned in the previous chapter, felt that this view was fundamentally flawed, was Martin Heidegger. He argued that when we position ourselves over and against the so-called objective world like this, objects and events can only be present remotely and in such a way that tends to eclipse the more primordial relationship that he believed we needed in order to truly appreciate and understand what is before us. He draws in the importance of things mattering to us by suggesting that an encounter with something is 'not a bare perceptual cognition, but ... the kind of concern which manipulates things and puts them to use; and this has its own kind of "knowledge"' (Heidegger, 1962: 67) Awareness of and responsiveness to the world becomes key and, crucially for Heidegger, this quality of awareness comes through, not just any casual experience but, more precisely, experience where we take time to attend and respond to the world – where we engage and genuinely immerse ourselves in the *use* of things.

EXPERIENCE, ENGAGEMENT AND ACTIVITY

Now this idea of not just standing over and observing the world but actively engaging with it suggests that we might want to attach importance to the very idea of activity. As we have seen historically, child-centred approaches have often called for practical activity to be at the heart of the curriculum. However, a call for corporeal and active engagement suggested in the previous chapter, allows us to see practice and activity in a different sense and it becomes possible to appreciate the extent of what could be at stake in this particular child-centred value. Heidegger builds on the idea of how multiple viewpoints and experiences enrich an individual's appreciation of an object by insisting that even the most mundane of objects in our experiences necessarily carry with them a sign-like quality. If we return to the image of the teacup placed on a table and remind ourselves that understanding requires experience and other viewpoints to augment our single perception, we need in particular an awareness of how a cup functions in our lives. For Heidegger, though, it is not only the simple function that a cup serves that is important for a genuine appreciation; we also need to appreciate the significance that it can have in lived experience and its relationship to other things. He would suggest therefore that to fully understand what a cup is, it should be seen as a sign, for it carries intrinsic reference to its uses and to other substances (tea, heat, saucer, teapot) as well as a capacity to draw forth awareness of previous experiences. For Heidegger, it is this sense of *significance* that gives the perception of an object its full meaning.

It might be helpful to illustrate this idea in Heidegger's own words. In his essay 'The origin of the work of art', he describes his response to Van Gogh's work entitled 'A *Pair of Shoes*' and takes great care to explain the significance that can be felt from a simple drawing of a humble pair of shoes:

'A Pair of Shoes' by Vincent Van Gogh (1853-1890). Reproduced with the permission of the Van Gogh Museum, Amsterdam.

> *There is nothing surrounding this pair of peasant shoes in or to which they might belong, only an undefined space. There are not even clods of soil from the field or the field-path sticking to them, which should at least hint at their use. A pair of peasant shoes and nothing more. And yet –*
>
> *From the dark opening of the worn insides of the shoes the toilsome tread of the worker stares forth. In the stiffly rugged*

heaviness of the shoes there is the accumulated tenacity of her slow trudge through the far-spreading and ever-uniform furrows of the field swept by a raw wind. On the leather lie the dampness and richness of the soil. Under the soles slides the loneliness of the field path as evening falls. In the shoes vibrates the silent call of the earth, its quiet gift of the ripening grain and its unexplained self-refusal in the fallow desolation of the wintry field. This equipment is pervaded by uncomplaining worry as to the certainty of bread, the wordless joy of having once more withstood want, the trembling before the impending childbed and shivering at the surrounding menace of death. This equipment belongs to the earth, and it is protected in the world of the peasant woman. (Heidegger, 1978: 160)

In Heidegger's account, a full and developed consciousness of the use of the shoes in such particularity, allows for the viewer to be open to what the shoes sign and call forth. A perceptive viewer then actively blends the image with all the feelings and understandings drawn from his or her own life, making connections with both real and imaginative experience. The drawing is obviously being considered primarily as a work of art and therefore perhaps naturally demands a high degree of close attention and we could argue that the sense of the drawing of the shoes as a 'sign' will be heightened. However, Heidegger suggests that attending in this way is an important and valuable method of relating and building understanding and appreciation of the world. The description he gives of this particular form of looking, with its depth of particularity and significance, can therefore be extended to experience and the world in general. From an educational point of view, the idea that a child needs to understand the world in which she or he finds themselves seems indisputable. However, to move from mere recognition and categorization of an object to this deeper and more extensive understanding would seem to involve drawing widely from a rich supply of everyday experience, connecting memories and prior understandings and perceptions, and attending closely and being receptive to the object itself.

The main point about this intensity of encounter is that it seems to exemplify engagement with the embodied mind – integrated senses, memories, thoughts and feelings are all gathered together and brought into play. In the case of the drawing, Heidegger is careful to explain that it is not the shoes themselves, but the physicality and concerns in the life of the peasant, *signed* by the shoes, that call forward the viewer's experience and understanding. In other words, the viewer perceives the significance of the shoes and in this way they acquire meaning.

SOME POSSIBLE IMPLICATIONS FOR EDUCATION

If we accept that a detached orientation to the world can impair meaningful thought and understanding, the alternative being offered here is to become immersed in life, to openly encounter objects and others that surround us – to fully participate and actively engage with them. The implication is that the deeper we are able to envelop ourselves in experience, the deeper our capacity to care for or value what we encounter, and the deeper our understanding and quality of thought. At the heart of the child-centred call for meaningful as opposed to detached learning, then, there is a claim that could be fleshed out by drawing on the ideas sketched above. If we feel that this characterization of how humans in fact strive to encounter the world rings true, then it would seem that education is best conducted through the development of understandings that the child genuinely feels have meaning and recalls the idea introduced by Rousseau, that necessity should drive what a child comes to know and understand. Education should not only be set within the experiential life

Remembrance: appreciating how other people felt and still feel about those that died in the war

world, but also encourage the child to stay receptive in certain ways and desire to become immersed in that world. In this way the child can continue to be active and discover and explore the personal significance of what she or he learns. There would be an important recognition that children can and should come to care about what they learn because it taps into the experience and understandings that they already own. In this way, their education can be driven forward by the developing values and concerns that really matter to them, for acknowledgement of this is essential if 'directives' are eventually to play such an important role in one's life.

> *A person's existence is an 'issue' for him, and in confronting it he must develop beliefs, values and interpretations of his situation, which will direct the shape he gives to his life. He must determine, for example, the place that work, pleasure or religion will occupy in his life; or the significance for him of, say, his membership of an ethnic group or a profession.* (Cooper, 1990: 114)

THE CRITICAL STANCE

We began this chapter by reminding ourselves of the predominant view of how humans should relate to the world that stresses objectivity. We pointed out that this has been criticized outside of education by philosophers who have tried to articulate a more embodied and embedded view of what it is to live in the world. It is important for our argument and concerns here that we also make explicit what may be at risk with the belief that a detached, analytical view of the world should be the main thrust for what ought to be transmitted through education. The main point is that many who stress the importance of children gaining objective knowledge, for instance, assume that a more detached view will necessarily give a *value-neutral* view of the world. Yet if we adopt a stance towards the world that is not only distant but also critical or analytical, our relationship to and apprehension of the world change. One illustration of this might be the so-called expert in any field of literature or the performing arts who has ceased to be able to immerse themselves in the rich experience of art or reading as a result of their highly developed critical consciousness. If the overriding orientation in our everyday lives becomes one of mastery and measurement, instead of the rich and receptive relationship that allows things to emerge and be revealed, the argument is that we become closed to the presence of things, and substances tend to lose their full sensuous weight for us and become levelled and perhaps even demeaned. For Heidegger, a dominance of this form of what he calls 'technology' inevitably leads to a sense that the world, its objects and above all meaning itself become diminished.

> *Heidegger goes beyond the banal romantic claim that technology objectifies and dominates nature. That is the way nature was treated during the rise of industrial production. Modern technology is something essentially different. It involves a new mode of revealing he calls enframing or ordering, which forces whatever is revealed to show up as ordered for use as a resource ... this new way [whereby] our practices order everything in our world shows us how our ... understanding is dedicated solely to the pursuit of efficient ordering merely for its own sake ... and levels those differences such as noble and ignoble, just and unjust ... which once gave meaning and direction to human activity in the West.* (Dreyfus and Hall, 1992: 13).

One example we can cite where new understandings and awareness have challenged an overly 'ordering' perspective is a more ecologically aware view of nature. Analysis, categorization and mastery has for centuries been the accepted view of how we should approach the physical world and also teach about the physical sciences. Recent climate and other ecological issues have fundamentally called this approach into question. It now seems rather an obvious and accepted idea that a detached and calculative view has allowed cumulative human action to exploit nature's resources and given us a diminished view of nature. The result has been the argument that greater value should be attached to the rhythms, beauty and power of nature and sense of place. With such a fundamental shift in perspective away from 'ordering', the very existence and certainly the fragility of the natural world can now be more widely appreciated than it once was.

It is worth stressing here that what has been described should not be seen as perpetuating another false dichotomy. It is not that objective, factual or scientific views of the world that are presented as 'true' or impartial should be completely replaced by the aesthetic, more subjective and emotional perspectives that are partisan and fundamentally not impartial in totality. Rather, what is being suggested is that the first view should not be seen as the *sole* perspective that education needs to develop in children to help them encounter the world in which they live. Nevertheless, the most important recognition we need to make is again how all developed understanding, including both objective and subjective, scientific and aesthetic, grows from the primordial relationship we drew attention to in Chapter 4. 'Our spontaneous experience of the world, charged with subjective, emotional, and intuitive content, remains the vital and dark ground of all our objectivity ... [and yet this] largely goes unnoticed or unacknowledged in scientific culture' (Abrams, 1996: 34).

Bonnett

One writer clearly influenced by Heidegger's ideas, who has recently developed and pursued the argument that an overly analytical view of nature carries risks, is Michael Bonnett. He argues that although 'there is an important sense in which nature constitutes our primordial reality' the predominant stance taken generally is one driven by 'an overweening motive for mastery' (Bonnett, 2004: 136). He goes on to argue that nature should be viewed in a more open and receptive way, giving us a sensibility which is fundamentally 'a condition of us having any meaningful experience whatever' (Bonnett, 2004: 137).

Another writer in this field, Charles Taylor, gives a similar warning:

> But we close ourselves ... when we turn away from living among things ... and identify them as context free objects, susceptible of scientific study ... even more so when we are swept up in the technological way of life and treat them as just standing reserve. If we make these our dominant stance to the world, then we abolish things, in a more fundamental sense than just smashing them to pieces, though that may follow. (Taylor, 1992: 265)

This may of course have direct implications for both what is taught within science in schools as well as the thinking that is encouraged alongside it. However, in an earlier book, Michael Bonnett deals more explicitly with the educational implications of seeing learning and teaching as involving the generation of a more objectified view of the world. In particular, he explores the implication for children's thinking, contrasting detached thinking, which he labels 'calculative', with a more personal, receptive way of encountering the world, that he calls 'poetic' thinking. Bonnett's basic criticism of a detached and critical stance towards the world is: 'its lack of appreciation of the importance of "subjective weight" in a person's understanding and general mode of relating to things, and its consequent overlooking of the role played by a person's own motivations in the meanings they are able to achieve in their thinking' (Bonnett, 1994: 97).

Now it is important to remind ourselves that these writers are not suggesting a stark dualism with reason on one side and passion on the other. The view we are developing does not dismiss all detached, critical thought and, indeed, many who claimed to be child-centred in their approach would, of course, argue that there must necessarily be a place for reason and the development of rational thought through education. However, the claim is that analytical thought is *secondary* and, while it has some value, that value is limited. In particular, just as emotions inevitably involve reason and elements of judgement and appraisal, so reason needs to remain 'meshed' and grow out of our direct encounters with the world. However, a detached and objective stance with an overemphasis on calculation and judgement can work against and take us away from the sense of ourselves as embodied and embedded in the world.

> *If our ... embodied engagement with a world ... 'opens' itself to us through our concerns and projects, there can be no reason to think that it will be disclosed only when we take stock and reflect. On the contrary, unless its features are revealed in a more 'proximal' way, there could be nothing to take stock of and reflect upon. If so, it must be wrong to suppose that reason is the faculty which discovers how the world is and passion merely the arena in which our subjective reactions to this discovery are played out.* (Cooper, 1990: 89)

For an education concerned with developing the whole child and encouraging meaningful learning, the implications are important. If thought and feeling ultimately only make sense through our continued physical engagement and meaning-making with the world, then educationalists need to understand the nature of this engagement. Experience involving the emotions, physical engagement and meaning-making becomes the priority and the form that education then takes must acknowledge and should reflect this.

We can again borrow some illustrations from Bonnett to specifically show what is at stake with the child-centred aspiration for encouraging learning that taps into a child's personal motivation and search for meaning. Bonnett sets out his characterization of calculative thinking and places it distinctively alongside the notion of poetic or meditative thinking not in the spirit of dualism but in the quest for clarity in our thinking about what is at stake for children. Bonnett's book as a whole is an unequivocal and well argued call for the

The rhythms of the seasons: planting bulbs to appreciate the effects we can have in the natural world

curriculum to redress the imbalance that has resulted from the dominance of the detached or rationalist orientation towards education and his summary of the contrasting features of poetic and calculative thinking is perhaps the best way to highlight this. He sets out a list to illustrate the contrasting stances towards things:

Calculative	*Poetic*
Self-purposeful	Celebratory
Goal-orientated	Openly curious, wondering
Analyses things into problems to be solved	Intuits the wholeness of things and receives them as they are
Turns things into defined objects – manageable, familiar	Stays with things in their inherent strangeness

Distinctions made in this way serve to illustrate the contrast between these two approaches and help us to see what a more embodied and embedded view of the child and her or his stance towards the world might look like. Furthermore we can see precisely to what it might stand as an antidote. On the one hand, we have the cultivated urge to sort and order the world and our experience within it, while on the other, we have a sense in which openness, and allowing ourselves to be affected by objects and events, will provoke awareness and feelings of care for the world.

There have been many criticisms of the current trends throughout education, those that reflect views of the child as future economic capital without regard to a child's present experience. In the general and perhaps global imperative to maximize the potential of each individual explicitly for society's needs, effort is made to prescribe what should be known in ways that often seem very akin to Bonnett's calculative way of looking at the world. The knowledge encapsulated in prescribed curricula is sometimes characterized more like information to be memorized and it is taught ('transmitted' is a term frequently used in relation to teachers delivering the curriculum) and layered upon the child, regardless of their interest or the relevance the content has to the child's own personal experience. Some educationalists and teachers have argued against this conceptualization and approach with the acknowledgement that a heavily prescribed curriculum must necessarily limit the extent to which individuals can find learning meaningful. Creative and imaginative teachers across the world working within prescribed systems like these, sometimes characterize their job as a struggle to try to 'engage' children more. However, the solutions to the problems that prescription has created that have been offered recently in Britain – the idea that we should 'personalize' the curriculum or make it more 'relevant' – have fallen into the trap of offering only partial or superficial antidotes. Personalization was characterized initially in the British government's 'Five Year Strategy for Children and Learners' (2004: 3–4), and the Minister for Education at that time, David Miliband, explained that it means: 'shaping teaching around the way different youngsters learn … [and] taking care to nurture the unique talents of every pupil' (Miliband, 2004). David Hopkins, Chief Adviser to Ministers on School Standards at the Department for Education and Skills (DfES) gave a justification for this move by claiming that: 'A system that responds to individual pupils by creating an education path that takes account of their needs, interests and aspirations will not only generate excellence, it will also make a strong contribution to equity and social justice' (Hopkins, 2005: 1).

However, as Robin Alexander has argued:

Alexander   *Big idea it may be, but as yet it remains opaque, despite its many airings. One such came in David Miliband's speech at the DfES/Demos/OECD conference on 18 May 2004. He started by saying what personalised learning is not:*

A return to child-centred theories.
About letting pupils learn on their own.
About abandoning the National Curriculum.
A licence to let pupils coast at their own pace.
Note the swipe at child-centredness to placate the right-wingers and
the derogatory equating of learning at one's own pace with 'coasting'.
It's hard to take seriously an account of personalised learning which
opens by dismissing the obvious truth that children don't all learn at
the same rate or in the same way. Or one which descends to the level
of a tabloid parody of 1970s educational thinking ... (Alexander,
2004: 24–5)

So, despite the rhetoric which could have heralded a change in vision
and might have seemed hopeful from a child-centred point of view,
it transpired that the new catchphrase of personalized learning was
more akin to individualizing the same 'calculative' curriculum
whereby the content just gets broken into more digestible chunks, or
perhaps the pace of expected acquisition is adjusted to children who
seem to learn at a slower rate than others (but not, note, their *own*
pace).

The second, more recent, idea of a *relevant* curriculum which, at
first sight, might appear to address the problems inherent in a curriculum comprising detached, prescribed content, may also disap-
point. In effect, 'relevance' may turn out to depend on helping
children see the point of their learning by steering lessons more
explicitly and securely to the 'real' world, that is, as adult conceptions
of the world of work. Without wishing to oversimplify the ideas here,
our main point is that solutions such as these may use child-centred
terminology but, with further examination, fall far short of tailoring
education to the whole person. We could suggest that much adult
malaise of disaffection, with its feeling of pointlessness and sense
that life has no meaning, may be the price that is eventually paid by
depending on this impoverished view of education. By misunder-
standing the fundamental problems with what we might call the age-
old, standard view of human encounter with the world, these kinds
of educational policies are oblivious to the central values and aspirations of child-centred education we have tried to flesh out in this,
and the previous, chapter.

The work of Merleau-Ponty and Heidegger cannot, of course, be
critically examined in any real philosophical depth within the space

we have here. As authors, we acknowledge that we have selected ideas from their work in order to give us glimpses and insights by philosophers that we feel are relevant to our purposes within this book. It is also important to stress that, while there are common themes that emerge from these and the other philosophers cited, there are also deep differences and distinctions that should be made between them if we were to do justice to the depth and extent of what lies further behind some of the ideas sketched. Nevertheless, these and other scholars have worked extensively to retrieve what they saw as neglected dimensions of human existence, and the fruits of their deliberations are worthy of consideration. The implications for education that can be drawn out of this discussion are, we believe, central to, and supportive of, a fuller understanding of some of the fundamental values that child-centredness espouses.

This chapter has picked up themes introduced previously in the book and has looked briefly at child-centred claims for 'active learning', 'relevance' and 'interests'. Its basic intention has been to argue that behind these terms of 'active learning', 'relevance' and 'interests' lies the more fundamental value best captured by the idea of pursuing learning that is meaningful. Nevertheless, meaningful learning is a vague and imprecise value, open among other things to extensive generalizations, so careful consideration is needed to see exactly what this might entail. The idea that learning can be genuinely felt as meaningful by a child was seen in turn as the kind of learning that carries subjective significance and weight for that child, and our suggestion has been that meaning will arise for an individual when personal involvement occurs and beliefs or values are engaged and meshed with the experiences offered in school.

The value of stressing that learning should be meaningful in the sense we have explored is that, in child-centred thinking, children can thus come to care about what they eventually know and understand. Perhaps at this stage we should stress the strength that this form of caring might take, for the claim is that 'directives' can generate both passion and strong beliefs. Our point would be that an overly prescribed curriculum, where one size is believed to fit all, is unlikely to generate the same degree of felt significance. Children come to learning with ideas, beliefs, imaginative associations, and aesthetic and moral values all engaged, and education should move them forward to maturity, keeping the child active in her or his own learning. In closing this chapter, we suggest that meaningful learning gives understanding that is deeply held and robustly attached to 'directives' and is much more likely to be, not only applied in real life but, more fundamentally, a guide to the personal actions and choices that constitute the business of life itself. It is in this way that we propose child-centredness asks that children should come to make sense of their learning and appreciate their education as 'relevant'.

FURTHER READING

Alexander, R. (2004) 'Excellence, enjoyment and personalized learning: a true foundation for choice?', *Education Review*, 18(1): 15–33.

Bailin, S. and Siegel, H. (2003) 'Critical thinking', in N. Blake, P. Smeyers, R. Smith, and P. Standish (eds), *The Blackwell Guide to the Philosophy of Education*. Oxford: Blackwell.

Bonnett, M. (1994) *Children's Thinking*. London: Cassell.

Dearden, R.F. (1968) *The Philosophy of Primary Education: An Introduction*. London: Routledge and Kegan Paul.

Taylor, C. (1991) *The Ethics of Authenticity*. Cambridge, MA: Harvard University Press.

Taylor, C. (1992) 'Heidegger, language, and ecology', in L. Dreyfus and H. Hall (eds), *Heidegger: A Critical Reader*. Oxford: Blackwell.

chapter 6

INTERDEPENDENCE: THE NEED FOR OTHERS

So far the values that we have discussed have stressed how any conception of what it is to educate needs to have at its heart, a comprehensive view of the whole child as a sensing and sense-making, embodied person. We have suggested that within a renewed child-centred view of education this would allow, in particular, more significance to be attached to each individual's immersion in their life-world of experience. Child-centred education would aim to encourage and support each child's search for meaning, thus strengthening their values, commitments and projects – their personal directives for engaging with life. All this necessarily focuses on the child as an individual. However, a closer examination of how understanding and significance are built up within a life-world can begin to highlight the importance of other, equally embedded and embodied persons, with their own perspectives, and it is to the relationship with these others that we now turn.

In Chapter 4 we suggested that multiple viewpoints are necessarily and largely already inherent within a singular perspective. A perspective in relation to the views of others is essential in order to prevent us developing unreliable and idiosyncratic understanding. Therefore we should understand how anyone comes to see and understand the world as a process whereby 'an intertwined matrix of sensations and perceptions, a collective field of experience lived through from many different angles [is built up and] ... sustained by continual encounter with others, with other embodied subjects, other centres of experience ... ' (Abrams, 1996: 39).

In Chapter 5 we extended and deepened this notion with the idea that fuller and more meaningful understanding can emerge when we appreciate the human 'significance' which is implicit in even the most simple of objects such as a cup or a pair of shoes. These ideas form the starting point for examining the extent to which an education that claims to both address the whole person and encourage meaningful learning, is dependent on relationships with others. It will therefore require a clear view of what kind of relationships can be seen to have value for child-centred education.

RELATIONS IN SCHOOL

Educational relationships are most clearly seen, of course, within schools. In fact schools are first and foremost collections of people: adults and children whose relationships are established and exist for a specific purpose – in order to educate the young. The conception that we have of what it means to educate will influence the nature of the relationships that evolve to achieve that purpose. Staying with the broader view of schools, it is interesting to note that some writers and theorists in education have sought to highlight the kinds of relationships education requires by advocating that we should see schools as *communities*, either for learning, or for enquiry. Views such as this arise from a belief that in very general terms, a community is best understood as a group of people united by an interest in developing shared ways of living. Those who claim we should see schools in this way argue that learning or enquiry should indeed be seen as a 'way of living' throughout a child's life in school. Furthermore it should then be seen to extend beyond the school and into later life – a way of seeing life as one centred around 'lifelong learning'. To make their nature clear, institutions described as communities are often contrasted with, and distinguished from, other groupings such as businesses, trade unions or committees because these kinds of groupings seem to come together for purely instrumental reasons and to serve very specific functions for individuals and society. The view that a school is a community may not explicitly claim to arise from a child-centred view of education but it contains emphases such as the shared understanding and engagement that echo some of the values we have been examining. Schools are described as communities springing from common understandings that provide members with a 'sense of identity, belonging, and involvement that results in the creation of tightly held webs of meaningful relationships that have moral overtones' (Sergiovanni, 2005: 55).

Sergiovanni

Sergiovanni is writing specifically about schools as communities and makes an interesting distinction between, on the one hand, learners and teachers who enter into a contract for learning and, on the other hand, those who enter into what he calls a 'covenant for learning'. This careful distinction is important for Sergiovanni because it binds the teacher and child together in a supposed agreement to teach and to learn. Not only that, but it sees both parties as needing to *commit* to the idea of learning and thus raises the 'value' dimension that he believes is necessary in an open relationship that acknowledges the power of harnessing the learners' own care for their learning. In a similar vein, another writer in this field advocates that schools should be seen as 'Communities of Commitment'

Senge

(Senge et al., 2000). Both of these writers go on to suggest that for schools to succeed as communities, the educational relationships between teachers and children in schools need to be described with the notion of learners and teachers as *persons* to the forefront. In other words, these relationships in schools should be seen in ethical rather than instrumental terms. We now examine what this might mean in the light of some of the child-centred values we have discussed previously. To do this we need to step out of the school context, back in to a view of life more generally.

PERSONS IN RELATION

When we reflect on the relationships experienced in life, there is a major distinction that is often made between those relationships that are seen as personal and those that are more instrumental. The latter appear to suit the many roles we take in life, and are seen to serve some kind of function in making our everyday lives work. These intrumental relationships probably characterize much of the social activity that is undertaken by us, they perform specific functions and are frequently directed to achieve particular, defined, purposes. We form functional relationships with taxi drivers and doctors, colleagues and clients. We also engage in more personal relationships where we sometimes speak of more freedom and inclination to reveal more of 'ourselves'. For some, these are extremely important, for it is only through personal relationships that we can have what we might call a personal life:

> we live as persons ... by entering into relationships with other people on a fully personal basis, in which we give ourselves to one another; or, to put the same thing the other way round, in which we accept one another freely for what we are, and in which therefore there is and can be no purpose other than the sharing of our lives ...
> (Macmurray, 1935: 54).

There is an important question to ask here about where we would wish to place teachers and learners in such a categorization. The fact that the teaching role is a professional one and has a clearly defined purpose which gives it meaning, implies that we should see the relationship between teachers and children as primarily functional. The very sense of teaching is constructed because we understand what it is to teach in relation to teaching some*thing* or some capacity and, importantly, some*one*. And if we accept this, we would need to say that by the same token, learners need to basically form functional relationships with their teachers. However, this immediately raises a tension with what has been discussed in our previous chapters. If child-centred education claims to see the child as a 'whole' person with due regard to the personal experiences of that child, surely the relationship between a teacher and child, defined by that form of education, must attend to more than the functional nature of the relationship? More specifically, the values evoked in the previous two chapters have suggested clearly that it is more important to have a strong sense of the personhood of the child, than an awareness of a simplistic view of their function or role.

For many, because functional suggests that we regard the relationship solely as a means to an end, the danger would be that this might allow us to slip into viewing the experience of the child and the child themselves in purely means/end terms. This is a view many would find uncomfortable when set alongside familiar ethical principles derived from Kantian thought. One imperative that many teachers would want to defend is the importance of respecting all persons as an end in themselves rather than a means to other ends. In other words, we should not *use* others to achieve our own ends however altruistic those ends might be. A familiar example of seeing persons as means might be a view of children and their achievements as important for the role they could play in elevating a school's position within league tables. This might manifest itself as a reluctance on the part of the school to admit children who were predicted to reach only low levels in standardized tests.

So we have revealed a tension here between the extent to which we need to see relationships as personal, based on a full sense of the person with whom we are engaged and the professional sense in which we need to hold the purpose or function of that relationship in the forefront of our thinking. This is perhaps a false dichotomy, whereby we might want to suggest that we should not think of the nature of relationships in terms of only one form or the other. The relationship between a teacher and learner clearly needs to be both professional and personal. The question is, exactly where along the continuum between these two versions would we want to place a child-centred view?

The stress on the importance of values and ethical considerations raised by the notion of community and personal relationships will easily resonate with someone who believes that the child should be viewed as a person who is considered, above all else, at the centre of their education. The brief conceptualizations of relationships and communities drawn from our selected writers in the field are useful for they point to ways in which a person-/child-centred education might manifest itself in school. The claim might be that although functionality and purpose are inevitable and must be taken into account, from a child-centred perspective the importance of the person must remain paramount. This would then offer a contrast with approaches to education in which the functional is allowed to dominate above the importance of the person. Despite these helpful distinctions we now need to see more explicitly how these ideas of relations to others can be tied into our earlier ideas of the whole child and meaningful learning.

ENCOUNTERING OTHERS

We need to return initially to the ideas about how humans encounter the world in which they live. If we want to be consistent with beliefs that education needs to support and encourage children to encounter the world in the whole-hearted, embodied and fully significant sense suggested earlier, what would this mean for their encounters with others? At one level we could make some general suggestions that relations might need to be democratic and responsive and quickly see that this would therefore require feelings of trust and mutual respect. But before we travel that route we need to exercise some caution. Too much stress on being open and receptive to the thoughts of others could also carry a risk, particularly to the young. Some of the writers already mentioned are wary of the demands we face in a social context and, indeed, urge that there are precious and hard-earned gains to be made by individuals who can resist the pressures from 'the crowd'. In particular, they suggest that what is at risk for an individual when they are swept along with the crowd, is the authentic development of their own 'directives'. In terms of schools, it is not only peer pressure that might be a problem; the powerful influence that even kindly teachers can have might also damage the fragile emergence of a child's authentic directives.

The risk being suggested here is not just in terms of being carried along mindlessly with the views of others; there is also a risk of others being capable of deriding or demeaning a person's genuine 'directives'. Cooper explains that:

> 'Possibilities' are the projects for lending shape to a life which a person determines in accordance with the beliefs and values that matter most to him. When these 'directives', and the 'possibilities' which they inform, are deprived of gravity by being treated as symptomatic of the person's group, class or character type, they are no longer his 'ownmost' ... Seen from the 'inside' his 'directives' are what give meaning to his life; viewed by the 'they', his 'directives' furnish meanings in the way hairstyles and jewellery do. His 'ownership' of his 'possibilities' is treated by the 'they' as akin to owning the watch or the wig that goes with his station or type. (Cooper, 1990: 116)

We might want to ask ourselves here whether teachers are capable of sometimes belittling a child's genuine concerns – dismissing them as maybe 'childish' in the rush to deliver and cover the stipulated curriculum for example?

Heidegger
Heidegger was one philosopher who believed that the strong pull we all feel, to be one with the crowd or subservient to the authority of another, helps us to hide from the real freedoms and choices we have. He addresses this problem through a detailed argument for the value of what he calls 'authenticity in relationships'. He argues that humans are 'thrown' into a communal existence initially and that the authentic life has to be 'won' (Heidegger, 1962: 126–30). The idea of an authentic life might seem to imply the need to be different and to

stand apart from others, but Heidegger's ideas offer a version of authentic relations that can exist within, and even contribute to, the creation of a community. His suggestion is that persons begin existence in relation to others and then need to strive towards authenticity, for in this way they are able to avoid assimilation into the crowd. Rather than severing relations, it is the *quality* of these relations which lies at the heart of authenticity and an understanding of what it is to coexist among others. Heidegger interprets the notion of quality and employs the idea of 'solicitude' or empathy to describe a person's general relation to others. He suggests that solicitude, giving deep attention and showing consideration and concern, should echo the care in our relationship to the world of constructs and things. Thus attentive consideration is important for it allows space for the integrity and genuine concerns or, in short, the directives of the other person to come forward. Heidegger refers to people being 'authentically bound together' when each 'frees the Other in his freedom for himself' (Heidegger, 1962: 122). Cooper speaks of being 'available' for the other and suggests this availability is of crucial importance and has to be seen as interpersonal, not something that can be achieved alone or simply as an intellectual exercise: 'Being available, which is never a solo feat, is participation in relations characterized by mutual "collaboration" with the freedom of each party' (Cooper, 1990: 178).

This all seems to chime neatly with the value given to the personal dimension in relationships, for we can only be authentically ourselves in relation to others when there is consistently true consideration and attentiveness that allows this to happen. A distinctive form of relationship then appears to be emerging for child-centred teachers – one way of relating to children that allows for open response and engagement but also, crucially, offers a 'clearing' between those engaged. In a mutual relationship based on solicitude, neither party leaps in to urge, dominate or disburden the other of her or his cares in the space between. Instead, a *clear* space is created that allows and even calls each person to articulate his or her own values and beliefs. Now this view may help in our understanding of personal relationships, but can it be valid for more educational relationships? In particular we need to note that relationships between children and teachers can never be equal in terms of authority and therefore the idea of mutual openness seems problematic. The argument would be that if education is to respect and enhance a child's awareness of their personal directives in the way that we have tried to suggest is central to very idea of what it is to truly educate, then teachers, as the main initiators, will need to cultivate relationships where there is the space for children to express and explore personal directives safely with others. Here the child-centred teacher would argue that the teacher–child relationship is pivotal in a school because it serves as the model for child to child relationships. In addition children in school are astute and more than able to observe and perceive the quality of relationships between adults. For this reason, adults within a school may need to be able to engage in a more fully mutual relationship. In part this will be again as a model for children, but also, as we argue in Chapter 7, as a way of refining their own personal and professional beliefs and values. This may be seen as one way for school staff to cultivate whole-hearted commitment to the directives that drive and characterize all the practice within that school.

ENCOUNTERS WITH TALK

We have now arrived at a characterization of the child at the centre of their life-world where, as well as their physical presence, objects and constructs are seen to feature all the resonance and human signification that comes attached to those objects and, furthermore, where an important part of that life-world consists of people. If the aim of child-centred education is the child's creation of meaningful understanding of their world and their experience, the suggestion is that this is developed through specific, authentic kinds of encounter with objects and people. The space to express and explore the things that matter to children will need to be created in ways designed to develop understanding in collaboration with others. The argument is that in the gradual and continual interaction with others we not only articulate and come to know what we experience but we grow confident that we can know and understand the world. 'It is this informing of my perceptions by the evident perceptions and sensations of other bodily entities that establishes, for me, the relative solidity and stability of the world' (Abrams, 1996: 39). But this is not about just giving time and space for talk and thought. Talk and thought of a particular quality are required.

Heidegger   It is worth highlighting two connections that can be made between talk and points raised in the earlier chapters. The first comes from Heidegger again. In his account of the importance we need to attach to the 'signification' of objects, he argues that the very language we all use is subject to, and in fact works through, the idea of 'sign'. He explains that words cannot be truly understood as separate entities or through simple objective definition. Instead, words are always encountered in use and are best understood within a web of reference. In practice, words are simply sounds but again, like objects, they develop meaning through human intention and use. The relationships and intuited sense of human experience called into being by a word or phrase is the same as the world called forth by the very presence of a simple cup. Both elicit that thick and rich world of experience that Heidegger believes ultimately nourishes and draws forth thinking, allowing us to increase our understanding.

Second, just as we have argued for an appreciation of the full corporeal sense of what it is to engage with experience, the activity of talking must be seen as part of this rich form of encounter. This fits well with our earlier account because talk draws heavily on the sights and sounds of body language for expression, so that discerning the meaning of another's utterance is a roundly sensual procedure. When we attend to someone speaking, we watch for expression including the kinetic actions they make and we listen to tone and inflection as well as (perhaps even prior to) the sense of the words being uttered (Doddington, 2001).

These points add coherence to the view that is being developed but there is a third important point. The analysis of the quality of talk that child-centredness may favour has something in common with the kinds of encounters with objects and others that we have been looking at. This feature is that all forms of what we might call child-centred encounters do not have predetermined outcomes. We have already discussed the limitations to the creation of meaning that might follow a tightly predetermined curriculum and, in a similar vein, if children are to seek meaningful learning and to own the understanding they gain through their encounters with others and the objective world, then there has to be a degree of both openness and open-endedness built into those encounters. In terms of language, one illustration of this might be the way in which we commonly acknowledge that we can use talk to articulate our thoughts, often forming those thoughts as we speak.

The suggestion is that there are certain kinds of tentative talk, where we feel we are able to use talk to clarify thoughts or feelings. Some have pointed out that this kind of talk is in effect not expressing preformed thoughts but is the means by which we are able to actually *constitute* those thoughts and feelings. If talk helps

Collective creativity: working together to make a collage

'me to have ideas, to find out what I want to say, as I say it, if it involves the expression and sharing of thoughts and emotions and the interpretation of others' expression, it is indispensable for personal meaning, human interaction and thought' (Doddington, 2001: 273). If this is the case, this is nowhere more important than with a child who might be engaged in activities and discussion in order to learn. From a child-centred perspective, this kind of experience is not only where thoughts are being formed, but also, over time, where interpretations are being shared to form meanings and understandings and where personal directives are being engaged. An educational context with ongoing relationships between a teacher and a child, as well as between children, would seem therefore to demand that interaction needs to possess some of this quality of talk. This means that the other crucial facet that we need to recognize in a relationship where the quality of attention and consideration implied by Heidegger's notion of 'solicitude' is valued, is the way in which persons are listened to.

the important thing ... is to listen to what (the other) has to say to us. To this end, openness is necessary. But this openness exists ultimately not only for the person to whom one listens, but rather anyone who listens is fundamentally open. Without this kind of openness to one another there is no genuine human relationship. (Gadamer, 1979: 324)

What is being introduced here is really a demand for considerate and attentive relationships that thrive on both the literal idea of talk and the idea of learning as if persons were engaged metaphorically, in a conversation.

Conversation is a process of coming to an understanding. It is characteristic of every true conversation that each opens himself to the other person, truly accepts his point of view as worthy of consideration and gets inside the other to such an extent that he understands not a particular individual, but what he says. (Gadamer, 1979: 385)

Grice   As Grice (1989) has pointed out, the value of conversation is that it is open-ended and cannot be predetermined but is disciplined or constrained by conventions. This demands that in child-centred education, children would be inducted into the conventions of genuine encounters through relationships endowed with a sense of mutual trust, and the willingness and opportunity to openly express authentic beliefs, values and interpretations through actions as well as words. In this way, there is the potential for directives to emerge or be reviewed in ways that generate meaning and understanding and gradually strengthen the sense and direction that a child wants to have in her or his life.

The introduction of the notion of conventions here is significant, for it implies that a child's ability to talk, or more broadly engage in all forms of expression, can benefit from the sophistications that human expression has achieved over the years. In a child-centred view this will not be achieved by a superimposed adult language – the vital importance of avoiding pre-specification remains. What would be coherent with this view is the idea of gradual absorption of developed forms of expression, sensitively introduced when appropriate by a teacher highly committed to preserving the importance of expression and meaning for that child. The writers that we have drawn upon are clear that sophisticated and shared communications are the sediments from continual exchange of idiosyncratic expressions. Therefore

> *With the 'sedimentation' of language, expression does not disappear, but now it utilizes words belonging to a relatively stable system. The grand testimony to this is the rhetorical and figurative power of language – its potential for metaphor, metonymy, irony, and the rest. In the exercise of this potential, words with more or less fixed meanings are put to novel work: the expression of individual visions, the inspiring of images, the prompting of unsuspected analogies and new classification.* (Cooper, 1990: 163)

Cooper

Cooper goes on to extend this beyond language to areas of human understanding such as morals and explains that morality too, cannot be prescribed – we have to derive the meaning of what is moral for ourselves, yet cannot innovate without the support of those ideas that are crystallized within the community in which we find ourselves. To this we might want to add many other forms of human achievement that are seen to progress and evolve over time including the ability to be creative and to mount enquiries in a range of fields.

CONCLUSION

This chapter has moved from consideration of the individual to the value of interdependence, for there is an important sense in which personhood is necessarily generated within social relationships. Some careful distinctions have been made to point out that child-centredness would need to reject a view of schools in terms of straightforwardly functional relationships collected into functional institutions. The suggestion emerged that, for example, a stress on community is one way to avoid an instrumental view of relationship and helps to capture a richer, multipurpose sense of education that could fit well within child-centred views of education. A related suggestion has been that relationships and the quality of linguistic interaction within those relationships need certain qualities if they are to fit in with the fundamental values that child-centredness holds dear. As in earlier chapters, we have stopped short of fully fleshing out some of the implications these kinds of values suggest for a current view of education. In our final chapter, we return to do precisely this on the basis of the historical lessons we have been able to learn from and the values so far set out in the book.

FURTHER READING

Alexander, R. (2001) *Culture and Pedagogy: International Comparisons in Primary Education.* Oxford: Blackwell.

Bruner, J. (1997) *The Culture of Education.* Cambridge, MA: Harvard University Press.

Doddington, C. (2001) 'Talk in the Classroom', *Studies in Philosophy of Education*, (INPE journal), March: 267–74.

part III

THE ROAD TO CHANGE

chapter 7

CHILDREN AND THEIR TEACHERS: THE CREATIVE TRADITION REVIVED

Bruner

Obviously there are no sure-fire answers. But there are certainly enough promising hints to encourage serious efforts. One of the most promising involves experiments in schools that have established 'mutual learning cultures.' Such classroom cultures are organised to model how the broader culture should work if it were operating at its best and liveliest and if it were concentrating on the task of education. There is mutual sharing of knowledge and ideas, mutual aid in mastering material, division of labour and exchange of roles, opportunity to reflect on the group's activities. That, in any case, is one possible version of 'culture at its best.' School, in such a dispensation, is conceived of both as an exercise in consciousness raising about the possibilities of communal mental activity, and as a means for acquiring knowledge and skill. The teacher is the enabler, primus inter pares. (Bruner, 1996: xiv)

Much of what we have written in this book will resonate with the ideas and beliefs of many teachers and those involved in education across the globe. Our intention has been to dig into the past and into philosophical ideas in ways which we believe make useful distinctions, explore connections and clarify concepts. The aim has been to therefore strengthen the debate about what the education of children should mean, and to influence the way it should be formed. In our previous chapters we have traced the lasting ideas embedded within historical expressions of child-centredness and clarified the values that lie at the core of those historical views. We have then explored key philosophical ideas and values within this vital legacy which we believe are worth taking forward to underpin educational practice in the twenty-first century. In this chapter we outline in more explicit ways how the practice of schools should be adapted in the light of our historical and philosophical analysis of child-centredness, forming, we hope, an encouragement to make some serious efforts towards improving the character of education now and into the future. By implication the chapter will continue to be, in part, a critique of some of the most prevalent educational ideas that currently hold sway in many international educational systems as well as in Britain. While the practices of education are most obviously found expressed in the activities and relationships forged within the classroom, we also intend to extend the ideas beyond this to the wider implications for whole school consideration. However, our main point remains, that this tradition gives autonomy back to the principal historical actors within education – the teachers and children. Thus, we argue, there is no totalizing prescription for curriculum and school 'effectiveness', but rather a call for a renewed emphasis on child and adult creativity in our schools rigorously conceptualized in terms of the values we have tried to highlight. In effect, we call for the political and educational decision-making that would aim to allow child-centred creativity to flourish once again.

CREATIVE AND MEANINGFUL EXPERIENCES: EMBODIED LEARNING

We believe that there are several features of learning that a child-centred approach to education would want to stress. The first is the value of what children, conceived of as persons in their own right, bring to their learning experiences in school. This central idea highlights not only the importance of teachers taking children's prior experiences into account, but also working with an understanding of how children encounter ideas, things and other people through their experience. A learning context that reflects this will need to mesh the present understandings of the child learner to explicit educational experiences that possess certain living qualities. Learning that is designed to do this is likely to give opportunities and activities that are sense based and may involve physical activity. Teachers will want to select and construct specific activities on the basis of their professional judgement, and these will be activities that are capable of capturing each child's bodily consciousness in ways that stimulate the kind of vibrant engagement that we have suggested is vital for deeper, more personal learning.

The kind of activities that would qualify for this form of learning are more straightforward than might first appear and it may help to make some concrete suggestions. For example, if we take the scientific notion of magnetism, there are, of course, a number of practical activities that children can undertake to experience and develop understanding using real magnets. However, to deepen understanding and awareness, young children might simply experience the idea bodily through collaborative movement, imagining they are being drawn or repelled across the room or even seated at their tables with hands illustrating the power of attraction, for example. With older children the same principle might apply by encouraging a basic sense of magnetism creatively represented through dance or dance-drama. In fact, the expression of abstract ideas through the senses and the body in order to find meaning in those ideas is a feature of arts-based activities that runs throughout human culture. Returning to scientific understanding in school, any activity based on a sense would need to involve the physical experience of that sense. In a very obvious way, learning about taste would have to involve the physical handling and tasting of things! As soon as we begin to list these features of learning, so valued from a child-centred perspective, there are tensions highlighted by the practical constraints in the current educational scene, constraints that seem to pull us away from these practical, concrete and creative ideas. In particular, physical and creative activities need much more time than, say, a simple demonstration or explanation of where on the tongue basic tastes are located or of what magnets do. The child-centred argument that we have constructed insists that these physical/intellectual experiences should take time precedence over the impetus to 'cover' curriculum content, because they acknowledge the depth of embodied learning. The power of bodily involvement in all aspects of learning should not be underestimated, as this example given by Jabadao in the National Avisory Committee on Creative and Cultural Education

(NACCE) publication *All Our Futures: Creativity, Culture and Education* shows:

> Susie attends a special school where she has a weekly session with a dance-movement specialist. Susie likes writing and has a lot to say. But her teachers can only read a portion of what she writes, because Susie doesn't notice the edge of the paper. As she writes, she works her way across the paper, then onto the desk, until she comes to the end of her reach. Then she returns to the page and starts all over again. No amount of talking about it made any difference; bigger paper doesn't help. Then her teacher asked the dance-movement specialist if she could help. They worked with an aspect of movement called 'flow'. It concerns the way a person allows energy to pass through and out of the body, or, at the other end of the spectrum, the way they hold it in. Susie moved with lots of 'free flow'. Her movement seemed to go on and on; if you clapped your hands and said stop, it took her a long time to come to some sort of stillness, but even then there was movement. Together they played 'flow' games; letting the energy go, then trying to stop it and hold it inside. Gradually the games moved closer to the skill of stopping at the end of the page. They played, move your arm against the floor and now 'stop!'. Susie returned to the classroom and never wrote off the paper again. She needed to learn this through her body, not her intellect. (NACCE, 1999: 37)

Although there is still a powerful tradition in early years education across the western world that the curriculum should be built around the child's direct sense experience of the material world, this wanes as the child grows older. As we have traced, since the Enlightenment and the subsequent establishment of 'Pestalozzian' education in the early infant schools in Britain, children under 7 years of age have been expected to play and learn through handling and examining coloured pictures, rags, buttons, toys, blocks, percussion instruments, natural objects and playground gardens. State infant schools did not in many cases realize this ideal, but it is fair to say that this vision of child-centred education has continued to challenge more regimented and formal visions of suitable education for the very young. Despite being constantly vilified and insidiously qualified, this tradition may still be recognized in a freer curriculum in the early years in primary schools. But clearly it withers as children pass the age of 6 or 7. In the teeth of the many research studies that have pointed to the value of immediate sensual experience when generating creative work by young children, studies that show, for example, that actually collecting, smelling, feeling and observing autumn leaves before writing autumn poetry, enriches the spirit, supports the child's entering into creative meaning in language, and thus elevates the quality of the child's writing.

Learning within a child-centred approach stresses that educational experiences should both challenge children intellectually and at the same time engage their emotions. However, this can be more complex than the illustrations offered above. As children grow and develop within their culture, they become increasingly aware that their experience of the world is communicated, not only through direct experience, but also through complicated systems of signs. They gather, and are shaped by, experiences that are in themselves representations. In other words, alongside their *real* and sensual experiences of the world run complex versions of *virtual* experience. Stories and pictures, for example, provide the growing child with alternative worlds that depend for their verisimilitude and their emotional impact on semiotic conventions, systems of symbol, gesture and sound. In reading a picture book or watching a film the learner has to have mastered not simply a series of decoding skills, but an understanding of the *symbolic* nature of different *systems of meaning*. And in order to make sense of, and to communicate with, different systems of meaning, learners must use the symbolic materials to construct ideas for themselves. It is here that the prescribed curriculum becomes too subject bound and skills based. The current descriptions of reading matter in the British National Curriculum, for example, which is an attempt to list important virtual experiences through literature, is far too prescriptive to be of much use in a multi-modal world that employs a range of semiotic systems. Many of the 'classic' books that teachers of literature and curriculum architects would see as essential reading are now widely available – and far more popular – as moving image texts. Other rich and meaningful texts are entirely pictorial, thus absent from the 'literature' curriculum altogether. Popular culture narratives, created and represented in animation and live action, moving image and comic book formats, are all again absent, leaving children's media experience out of school. Thus a meaningful, child-centred curriculum would not only ground creativity in real experience but also acknowledge a more sympathetic categorization of the child's *virtual* experience – one that would span across semiotic systems, garnering experiences within the multiple ways that the communicative technologies now function in our culture. Here, embodied learning experiences would challenge children intellectually by engaging their emotions. More familiar examples of blending ideas across systems of meaning might be the use of the poetry of Wilfred Owen to shed light on the felt experience of foot soldiers in the First World War, or role-play and other drama activities designed to elicit the feelings and experiences of wartime evacuees in the early 1940s.

Another theme that has emerged throughout our chapters is the importance of learning that in some way relates to a child's directives, her or his personal beliefs and values. Opportunities for the authentic engagement of these beliefs and values need to be sought by both teacher and learner. The activities, and the thoughts and actions they encourage, need to offer the chance to share and refine and develop the things that really matter to children. Here stories and texts can grip to an extraordinary effect. While a teacher has to bear this requirement for deep engagement in mind in decisions and selections made with texts and ideas, it is worth pointing out that not even the person involved can always predict what will touch them in any degree of depth. Even for ourselves, as adults, there is a limit to how much we can pre-plan this kind of deep engagement. Although guided by titles or reviews, in watching a film or reading a book adults may totally unexpectedly find resonance with their own predicaments and values. For children, their own or their teacher's choice of poem or a picture book may be a guide or a starting point, but there is no guarantee that the text chosen will resonate fully with each and every child. Take for example, the picture book by John Burningham entitled *Granpa* (1984). The human truths that can be found here range between the recognition of the everyday experiences of children found in the book's illustrations of domestic activities, and the playful relationship that the protagonist child has with her grandfather, but they can also extend to recognition of a sense of loss and the meaning of death. Any reader, of any age, can pour his or her own sense of life experience into the space created by Granpa's empty chair.

Another dimension of 'living' experiences that can constitute learning is instated by encouraging a child to experience in the present and at the same time look both to the past and to the future for meaning. By this we mean the process of recognizing the importance of insight that can grow from expressing or reflecting on previously acquired understanding during present learning experiences – of learning something that we already know. A teacher who appreciates that learning is not a simple linear process will be sensitive to the importance of challenging or retrieving assumptions and knowledge that the child already holds. At the same time, in terms of the future, the idea would be to look to learning that stimulates a child's own sense of agency. This means learning experiences that allow the child the opportunity to make choices and take initiatives concerning their lives and the learning projects being undertaken as well as those that might lie ahead. An example of how this might work in practice could involve the setting up of whole-class role-play contexts where children, representing different roles within a community or village in the past, improvise meetings or other events where new challenges arise. Perhaps the created community is faced with the threat of the addition of a new runway to the local airport, or the village fears being invaded by the king's army during the English civil war. In this imaginative context, sensitively managed by the teacher, children can develop roles that draw on the knowledge they have – of how people conduct themselves in meetings, or what the conditions might have been like in rural communities at times during the past. These understandings can, of course, come from books, personal experience or television, but they are drawn into the enactment as children emotionally engage with their predicament and develop their roles in relation to others who are also engaged. As tension mounts, with problems being revealed perhaps by the teacher also taking a role within the drama, the children can be faced with dilemmas, decisions and choices that feel 'real'. By being engaged in role, the predicaments that are being faced by children begin to matter to them – they start to care about what is going to happen.

Drama is a particularly good example to illustrate this kind of learning experience because children have a natural capacity for imaginative play and representation of others. The emotional, intellectual and physical embodiment of a role highlights the totality of engagement that a child-centred approach aims for. However, other forms of imaginative contexts, such as using puppets or creative open-writing tasks, can also call forth this quality of deeply intuitive engagement. Here it must be recognized that different forms of engagement with ideas demand different forms of response. At one end of a possible spectrum, when children engage and create almost entirely through processes of intuition, something deep and complex happens that is almost impossible to unravel through language. Reflection by the child and by any outsider to his or her act of creativity, must in this case respect the way that the brain can 'catch fire' – alighting a deeply subconscious and intuitive impulse across the mind. A child of 6 years once produced a stunning abstract painting and on being asked how she had produced it she replied 'I let my imagination run riot'. Here the act of reflection by teacher and child must be sensitively shaped by the very intuitive and holistic nature of the creative act. At the other end of this spectrum, where a child engages with processes and the products that are symbolically and logically related to recognizable texts and cultural forms, usually within a genre structure, the child's engagement is to some extent analysable, open to shared reflection, potentially dialogic in its use of a specific communicative technology and the rules and conventions that it invokes and reinterprets. Here a mediating 'play' of interaction and conversation by teacher and child enhances the learning in important ways. They engage in dialogue, analysis, suggestion and challenge. It must be stressed therefore that different forms of engagement and creativity require very different acts of reflection. Within a child-centred approach a range of forms of engagement and creativity are recognized and respected through the ongoing process of creativity and of reflection.

PLAY

Gadamer   The argument for the educational value of play has been rehearsed in many contexts, particularly in early years education. However, there are particular features of play that need attention here to point out the relevance of play to child-centred educational experience more broadly. Playful activity can generate reflection and understanding for the participant, but is also beneficial as a release from reality. The philosopher Hans Georges Gadamer suggests that: 'The structure of play absorbs the player into itself and thus frees him from the burden of taking the initiative which constitutes the actual strain of existence' (Gadamer, 1979: 105). Gadamer's analysis is interesting in that he argues that play necessarily needs freedom from the imperatives of the urgent or mundane and has to occur in an alternative, constructed reality. Even as adults, when we play a game, the player has to be willing to slip into an alternative, constructed world and to submit to that world's own particular rules in order to make the game work. Gadamer argues that in an imaginative context, this release is vital to give us the freedom that allows us to 'play with ideas' or entertain possibilities, to suppose or to imagine. Just as the rules of the game enable that game to proceed and take place, so the conventions that structure any experience we might call play are important, particularly if the play is collaborative. These two constitutive features – release from reality and structure through conventions – continue to be important in more sophisticated expressions of the imagination and play such as in the performing arts.

Passmore   Nevertheless, the state of being in play is a vulnerable one. The philosopher John Passmore, in his analysis of what constitutes a game, warns that any game will 'turn into toil if the element of play is ever removed from it' (Passmore, 1980: 240). Similarly, the fragile, imaginary world of a picture book can be diminished without a genuine space for this important sense of 'playing in an alternative world'. To put this more pertinently, the systematic analysis of sounds and practice in decoding that is often the central objective of many a picture book-based literacy lesson, may turn play into toil and destroy the very point of literature. The argument is that room for playfulness with its requirement for release from the imperatives of the so-called 'real' world then needs to be preserved in a child-centred context where the aspiration is for meaningful learning.

To make the point about play more clearly, it will be helpful to distinguish between imaginative activity and purposeful deceit. Consider what occurs when children are engaged in imaginative play:

A child make-believing he is a bear is not trying to deceive as a liar tries to deceive us; he is pretending to be sure, but not as a confidence-man pretends. By the very act of stepping on to a stage – as distinct from a platform – an actor differentiates himself from a mountebank ... a lying politician. (Passmore, 1980: 240).

Gadamer cites Aristotle who makes a similar point:

> ...when children enjoy dressing up, as Aristotle remarks, they are not trying to hide themselves, pretending to be something else in order to be discovered and recognised behind it; but on the contrary, they intend a representation. The child wants at any cost to avoid being discovered behind his disguise. He intends that what he represents should exist, and if something is to be guessed, then this is it. We are supposed to recognise what it 'is'.
> (Gadamer, 1979: 113)

These references are simple to relate to the physical involvement of drama experiences within education for children, but are also relevant in a broader sense. The assumption that play and the arts do not deal with reality but instead deal only in fantasy is a misapprehension that thwarts any argument for the value of these activities in education, particularly an education that aims at generating meaning for the learner. Many philosophers and educationalists would challenge that assumption as the quotations above begin to suggest. Imaginative worlds are not divorced from reality but often lift us above the mundane in order to understand and reflect back upon our 'reality'. It could be argued that the popularity of fantasy fiction such as Harry Potter and the Philip Pullman trilogy *His Dark Materials* (2001) stems not from the fanciful settings, costumes and fantastical events, but that the real draw for readers lies instead in the vivid truths concerning feelings and motivation that children and adults recognize and find within the accepted conventions of character, setting and story. Indeed these are truths which maybe could not be approached so clearly or so well without a fictional context and those conventions.

There are now other conventions that the twenty-first century has opened up that richly extend the resources of play and the arts, including fiction. Education has been slow to recognize this, in part because of the very misapprehension we have mentioned that neglects the importance and value of truth-seeking in imaginative or creative activities. The new technologies – particularly digital technologies – both stimulate and express children's instinct to play and to create. These now allow an extraordinary mixing of forms. Older hierarchies and conventions in the arts are giving way to new postmodern heterogeneity and reconceptualization. Imaginative and affective uses of the new technologies support a mixing and blurring of cultural forms.

Yet this dynamic, creative, and corrosive phenomenon, everywhere apparent, makes a spectacular contrast to the British national curriculum with its literal, monocultural and subject-specific design. Indeed, currently in Britain, in the effort to control education through targets and accountability, the National Curriculum provides the most detailed, instrumental and narrowly defined list of subjects and skills perhaps ever conceived, all of which enclose and formalize 'school learning' even for the youngest children. The time and space needed to play and, most importantly, to create, in all areas of the curriculum, have become diminished and undervalued. Emphasis on subject boundaries, skills and assessment have meant that drawing, painting, dancing, performing and playing music, instead of flowing across the time and space of the school day, are prescriptively subordinated to a traditional subject taxonomy. At the same time, the new technologies, while given a new and important status in *functional* terms, have been completely ignored in *aesthetic* fields. Children's media experience, for example, is virtually invisible in the National Curriculum. There is almost no recognition that their lives are given aesthetic depth and richness through television, video, computer games, art programmes, through home-based performance and music from electronic sources, and through multimedia texts and authoring now available to play with.

However, this situation has given rise to a fascinating culture of independence amongst even the youngest children. New technologies allow a freedom, hitherto impossible to achieve, to mix, overlap and subvert cultural forms. The child's instinct to play, and to create, has moved outside the classroom into invisible spaces of private homes so that, damagingly, the new kind of play allowed and validated by their extraordinary creative competence with multimedia technologies is no longer engaged with children's learning in school. Here teachers desperately need time and space to reflect. If our young pupils are even more technically competent than we are, moving across the world of visual representation, performance, moving image and musical composition in ways that almost beggar belief, then can we present them with a curriculum that is an insult to their creative imaginations? The very intensity of encounter with ideas that the child-centred tradition offers is currently lost in a mass of rigid curriculum prescription.

THE NATURE OF TEACHING

A consideration of the nature of learning based on the ideas, principles and values that we have explored as central to a child-centred approach, leads us by implication to consider the role of the teacher. It is clear that the teacher in these learning experiences cannot be just a bystander. Instead, in the child-centred tradition, the role of the teacher is conceived of as a sensitive and supportive intervener with clear commitment and appreciation of how to work out the principles and values in their own particular teaching and learning contexts for maximum benefit for each child. The teacher must have personal expertise in order to use possible curriculum content to offer a resource and framework for learning experiences. However, teachers do not just need subject knowledge but must themselves own a rich, experiential and cultural life from which to draw in their renewed capacity in their work to express their own values and creativity. Hence teachers need educating, not simply training. This is vitally recognized in other cultural environments. In Portugal, for example, teachers have free passes to all art galleries and museums, and Australasia and America offer bursaries to practising teachers for travel and study abroad.

The extent to which the teacher will need to plan and maintain professional oversight of the directions in which children's learning develops will also be key to the coherence and consistency of how children progress. It is important to acknowledge the space, time and insight needed to flexibly manage the complexity of what is envisaged here. It will require judgement and the opportunity for autonomy that many of the current constraints in education systems seem to seek to curtail. In the thrust for centralized prescription or control and accountability through measurement there is now a vast plethora of instructions for what teachers should do: exactly what they should teach and the way they should teach it. One of the underlying themes of this book is that in order to make good professional judgements for the children they know, it is vitally important for teachers to be aware of and committed to the ideas and values that inform *why* a teacher should teach something and *why* they should then choose to teach in a particular way, rather than simply the *what* they should teach or the *how*. Good teaching is necessarily a highly practical form of work but it needs also to be an intellectually rigorous and value-informed practice.

One of the starkest errors in the current educational world is the assumption that measured performance is the key to both monitoring and informing the planning for educational practice, and therefore in turn the means by which measurable standards can be raised. Quite simply, what can be measured may not be the most important things that children can learn an, correspondingly, some of the richest experiences that we are claiming are central to quality learning may defy simplistic measurement. On the other hand, there is much that teachers need to know about children in order to construct a context for learning that offers the many opportunities we have tried to outline. Beyond the restricted labels of class, race, gender and ability, there is the richer knowledge of them as persons in the ways we have suggested. Some awareness of their lives, experiences, concerns and values would help to understand something of the 'directives' that we have suggested are so important for making learning meaningful. Yet undoubtedly the pressures are currently for teachers to ascertain ability through testing, and then use this as the single most important determinant of planned individualized learning programmes (so-called 'personalized' learning). On this reductive model of conceptualizing the child, even race, class and gender become invisible and are to be ignored so that knowledge of the child is reduced to knowing only his or her measured levels of performance in set tests.

The cost of this prevalent view to children's education has recently been explored in a research project entitled 'Learning without Limits'. In this project, secondary and primary phase teachers in England, who were interested in working in classrooms in ways that did not revolve around the limitations that ability labelling places on children, experimented with different ways of organizing learning. The results were interesting and the effects recorded by teachers and children were salutary. In terms of our argument here, one of the most important aspects was the difference that children detected in their own and their teacher's commitment to learning. Our proposed emphasis on choice featured significantly for some young people who were interviewed:

> One Year 10 girl said that it made a difference to her to feel respected by the teacher, as it made her feel like 'giving more to the lesson'. The opportunity to choose between different tasks and activities was also identified as being important in generating

greater feelings of commitment. As one person commented, 'Since I chose what I wanted to do, I had to work harder on that.'
Although the young people did not use the word commitment, they seemed to imply it as they spoke about the importance of the feeling of being known, cared for and responded to as an individual. (Hart et al., 2004: 218)

With this broader conception of what it might be to 'know' the children you teach, teachers would need to forge relationships that constituted some of the values we outlined in Chapter 6. We suggested that space was required in the relationship between teacher and child that would encourage and allow children to express themselves authentically. One of the keys to this, we suggested, was a quality of listening that teachers could engage children with. Again this was a feature of the child's perspective that emerged in the 'Learning without Limits' project. Some of the interviews indicated how important teachers who listened were for the children involved in the project:

The importance of the teacher genuinely listening and paying attention to young people's ideas was a recurring theme across the interviews. The young people contrasted genuine listening with pseudo-listening; as one student put it, 'You have got something to say and the teacher is going "yep, yep" and they are not listening to you. It's like you are in your own little world and no one can see you.' When they felt that teachers were genuinely listening, and using their ideas to contribute to the lesson, this reinforced their commitment to the learning of the whole group and their sense of the value of what they had to offer. (Hart et al., 2004: 218)

It seems that some of the features we have highlighted have a significance for children's learning that they themselves are able to identify, not least when the feature they consider important is missing. Teachers' knowledge of children is significant, but it is how they then use and show that knowledge that counts from the child's perspective. Again, here are the children's voices from the 'Learning without Limits' project:

Closely linked to this sense of being known, respected and listened to attentively was a sense that the teacher cares. Care breeds trust, as one Year 10 student commented: 'You need to know he cares about your work ... we trust him.' This sense of care is noteworthy precisely because young people know only too well that it cannot be taken for granted. They know classrooms where it is absent, and that its absence generates fear and inhibits engagement. In such classrooms, they maintain distance and try to avoid notice, rather than actively seeking interaction with the teacher to exchange ideas, ask questions and have their thinking challenged and extended. (Hart et al., 2004: 218)

Careful listening as we hear each others' thoughts about the morning's activities

CREATIVITY IN SCHOOL: REVIVING A PROFESSIONAL CULTURE BASED ON BELIEFS AND VALUES

So far in this chapter we have discussed the nature of learning, the curriculum and the role of the teacher in forging relationships. While it is not possible to examine all the implications that might follow from adhering to child-centred educational values, the intention has been to offer some possible illustrations. The point we need to reiterate, however, is that practice cannot be prescribed but will follow from certain educational principles and values held by the teachers and adjusted to specific circumstances. Detailed practice then will need to be largely designed at the point of actualization, where teachers can interpret and make judgements with a full understanding of the context in which they work. Thus, in child-centred education the act of reflection holds within itself seeds of change and transformation. Reflective practice in school or work-place moves the whole vision of teaching and learning to a new intellectual space. In this approach, for the reflective practitioner, the learning child, the curriculum, the school day and the nature of creativity itself can move into the spotlight and become subject to change. In this more intense gaze the larger questions soon arise. What are we trying to do as educators? What is the nature of childhood and learning? What are the values on which we base our practice? It is these processes of reflection that allow teachers to examine possible transformations of pupil and teacher creativity within the larger picture of primary education, enhancing their professionalism and strengthening their own creativity.

Teachers who are working in this reflective way do not just draw on preformed understandings as they work. We suggested in Chapter 6 that language and other forms of expression actually constitute thoughts and feelings, and we wish to extend this to professional discourse. Teachers plan, reflect, talk with colleagues and articulate those plans into learning encounters for children. We believe that this professional form of experience helps to build knowledge and deepen understanding. Given sufficient autonomy, teachers can make selections in their approach to material taught, construct views of learners and make judgements about how learners respond. They will make choices about the ways that the policies of the school can influence and be expressed through practice. From a child-centred perspective teachers generally will need to strive to articulate practice in ways that are coherent in terms of the learning, embodied and playful child, constructing meaningful experiences and entering into reflective dialogue with young learners, with colleagues and parents.

Teaching is often presented as simply making rational decisions about practice, like choosing which pupils work together, what method to employ, or what activity to introduce. But none of these kinds of decisions are merely practical or free-standing choices. The validity of any professional decision is judged, not just by the outcome, but in part by the values and beliefs that are assumed or held. However minor, the child-centred approach demands constant and fluid review and modification by teachers as a key feature of the ongoing practice in every classroom. Hence teachers become engaged in an exciting process whereby they continually question, interpret and evaluate to understand what should happen next. This process is far more complex than the simple idea of making choices and decisions suggests. As predictable and rule-governed as some might wish teaching to be, the essentially human and person-to-person nature of teaching means it can never be preordained to the extent suggested by a discourse that implies that effectiveness is the only criterion we should use to evaluate teaching.

The picture we are constructing of teachers implies a degree of professional commitment that can be detected in many classrooms and also in the accounts given by our two teachers in Chapter 2. Teachers who have come to care deeply about education, may find that the formation of personal 'directives' is intimately connected to the values and assumptions they hold about education. Jennifer Nias found that about an eighth of the teachers she interviewed 'were actively concerned to create, through their teaching, a more *Nias* humane, socially just and constructively self-critical world' (Nias, 1989: 33). These kinds of beliefs form a backcloth to teaching and can contribute to a flexible framework for practice. The freedom and space to collaborate in disclosing and refining professional issues and acts which shape values could thus be personally significant, tied to the beliefs and concerns in life that teachers hold most deeply, those that are perhaps central to their identity. Woods and Orlik (1994) found the negative experience of inspections left some teachers demoralized and questioning themselves deeply: 'I find myself thinking, "What's my purpose? What's my role?" ... It goes right down to where you see yourself in the scheme of things and what's important.' A further question emerges when reflecting on some of these points. Could the current state of haemorrhage from the teaching profession by young teachers in their first years be partly explained by them entering the profession believing that their beliefs and deeply held views will find expression in their work, and instead finding the work overly instrumental and heavily prescribed in ways that obstruct this form of reflection and practice?

THE POLITICAL WILL FOR CHANGE

> *When and if we pass beyond the unspoken despair in which we are now living, when we feel we are again able to control the race to destruction, a new breed of developmental theory is likely to arise. It will be motivated by the question of how to create a new generation that can prevent the world from dissolving into chaos and destroying itself. I think that its central technical concern will be how to create in the young an appreciation of the fact that many worlds are possible, that meaning and reality are created not discovered, that negotiation is the art of constructing new meanings by which individuals can regulate their relations with each other.* (Bruner, 1986: 149)

Where do we go from here? In this book we have traced the child-centred tradition from its Enlightenment origins, setting it out in broad terms as a vital historical and philosophical alternative to those who view the education of the nation's children as an instrumental and authoritarian process. We have argued that the deeper engagement with the whole embodied child through meaningful experiences that respect the child's own directives is a happier and more creative challenge for teachers as well as their young pupils. Getting inside this philosophical, yet practical, tradition enables us to see very clearly how cruelly narrow and mechanistic much educational practice has recently become in many primary schools. The insistence of successive governments on seeing children as merely future economic actors has leached away the opportunities for creative engagement between teacher and pupil.

Only a wide-ranging national debate on childhood and school will generate the political will for change – and that change has to accept that teaching and learning in the primary school must be radically revised. Parents, teachers, school governors and local authority officers will need to rediscover their own voices and powers so that authority can work upwards from the classroom to central government, ensuring policy is based on, and furthers, good practice. It will be found necessary once again to restructure the curriculum and the school day around wide-based themes and genres, which are designed to foster the interests and the whole embodied experiences of all children. Rather than the current focus on ever narrowing learning objectives and lower-order skills, higher-order cognitive skills based on direct physical experience, on powerful texts and ideas, skills such as comprehension, enactment, and the expression and enrichment of individual voice, would be the main aims for all children. Children's experiences of life, of literature and moving image, play and meaning-making, would be recognized, respected and creatively utilized in school. Here play, enactment, reflective discussion and fully embodied learning would allow a deep play with meanings and ideas that would naturally move across and through separate subjects. Indeed, the primary curriculum would be released from its straitjacket of subject taxonomies so that children's aesthetic instincts can lead to an active hybridism of texts and ideas. For teachers and other adults involved in educating children, the implications that follow from the vision we have tried to articulate include a revised professional role where personhood is highly regarded. Adults as partners and colleagues would need to be engaged in authentic, interpretative working relations, with value placed on the quality of critical and creative dialogue that is generated. The practice of open engagement that allows for expression of values, beliefs and interpretations has the potential to reverberate throughout the community of a school for both adults and children. In this long-valued, child-centred, creative and experimental tradition the teachers' own creative instincts would necessarily be encouraged and enriched so that the work of teaching children would once again become pleasurable and fulfilling. Our children would be given the chance to create the possible worlds that would help with ensuring the survival and enhancement of this one.

bibliography

Abrams, D. (1996) *The Spell of the Sensuous*. New York: Pantheon Books.

Alexander, R. (2001) *Culture and Pedagogy: International Comparisons in Primary Education*. Oxford: Blackwell.

Alexander, R. (2004) 'Excellence, enjoyment and personalized learning: a true foundation for choice?,' *Education Review*, 18(1): 15–33.

Allen, A.T. (1982) 'Spiritual motherhood: German feminists and the kindergarten movement, 1848–1911', *History of Education Quarterly*, 22: 319–39.

Bailin, S. and Siegel, H. (2003) 'Critical thinking', in N. Blake, P. Smeyers, R. Smith and P. Standish (eds), *The Blackwell Guide to the Philosophy of Education*. Oxford: Blackwell. pp. 181–93.

Best, D. (1992) *The Rationality of Feeling: Understanding the Arts in Education*. London: Falmer Press.

Bonnett, M. (1994) *Children's Thinking*. London: Cassell.

Bonnett, M. (1996) 'New ERA values and the teacher–pupil relationship as a form of the poetic', *British Journal of Educational Studies*, 44 (1): 27–41.

Bonnett, M. (2004) *Retrieving Nature*. Oxford: Blackwell.

Bourdieu, P. and Passeron, J.C. (1977) *Reproduction in Education, Society and Culture*. 2nd edn. London: Sage.

Brehony, K. (2000) 'English revisionist Froebelians and the schooling of the urban poor', in M. Hilton and P. Hirsch (eds), *Practical Visionaries: Women, Education and Social Progress 1790–1930*. Harlow: Pearson. pp. 183–200.

Bruner, J. (1986) *Actual Minds, Possible Worlds*. Cambridge, MA: Harvard University Press.

Bruner, J. (1996) *The Culture of Education.* Cambridge, MA: Harvard University Press.

Burningham, J. (1984) *Granpa.* London: Jonathan Cape.

Butler, M. (1972) *Maria Edgeworth: A Literary Biography.* Oxford: Clarendon Press.

Carpenter, M. (1853) *Juvenile Delinquents: Their Condition and Treatment.* London: W. & F.G. Cash.

Carr, D. (1999) *Professionalism and Ethics in Teaching.* London: Routledge.

Carr, W. (1995) 'Education and democracy: confronting the postmodernist challenge', *Journal of Philosophy of Education Society of Great Britain,* 29 (1): 79–92.

Clarke, D. (1965) *The Ingenious Mr Edgeworth.* London: Oldbourne Book Co.

Clarke, K. (1985) 'Public and private children: infant education in the 1820s and 1830s', in C. Steedman, C. Urwin and V. Walkerdine (eds), *Language, Gender and Childhood.* London: Routledge and Kegan Paul. pp. 74–87.

Cooper, D. (1990) *Existentialism: A Reconstruction.* Oxford: Blackwell.

Cox, C.B. and Dyson, A.E. (eds) (1971) *The Black Papers on Education.* London: Davis-Poynter Ltd.

Cunningham, P. (1988) *Curriculum Change in the Primary School Since 1945: Dissemination of the Progressive Ideal.* Lewes: Falmer Press.

Darling, J. (1994) *Child-Centred Education and its Critics.* London: Paul Chapman Publishing.

Dearden, R.F. (1986) *The Philosophy of Primary Education: An Introduction.* London: Routledge and Kegan Paul.

Department for Education and Skills (DfES) (2004) *Five Year Strategy for Children and Learners.* London: The Stationery Office.

Dewey, J. (1934) *Art As Experience.* New York: Minton Balch and Co.

Dewey, J. (1938) *Experience and Education.* London: Collier-Macmillan.

Dickens, C. (1854) *Hard Times.* London. This edition Oxford University Press, Oxford, 1955.

Doddington, C. (2000) 'Editorial', *Education 3–13,* 28 (October): 2–4.

Doddington, C. (2001) 'Talk in the classroom', *Studies in Philosophy of Education,* INPE journal, March: 267–74.

Dreyfus, H. and Hall, H. (eds) (1992) *Heidegger: A Critical Reader.* Oxford: Blackwell.

Drummond, M.J. (1993) *Assessing Children's Learning.* London: David Fulton.

Dunne, J. (1993) *Back to the Rough Ground.* Notre Dame, IN: University of Notre Dame Press.

Edgeworth, M. and Edgeworth, R.L. (1798) *Practical Education.* London: J. Johnson.

Elliot, R.K. (1998) 'Versions of creativity', in P.H. Hirst and P. White (eds), *Philosophy of Education: Major Themes in the Analytic Tradition.* (4 vols.) London: Routledge. Vol. 2, pp. 224–33.

Ezell, M.J.M. (1983) 'John Locke's images of childhood: early eighteenth-century response to *Some Thoughts concerning Education*', *Eighteenth-Century Studies*, 17: 150–5.

Fielding, M. (1999) 'Target setting, policy pathology and student perspectives: learning to labour in new times', *Cambridge Journal of Education*, 29 (2): 277–89.

Fielding, M. (2000) 'Community, philosophy & education policy: against the immiseration of contemporary schooling', *Journal of Education Policy*, 15 (4): 397–415.

Fitz J., Davies, B. and Evans, J. (2006) *Educational Policy and Social Reproduction: Class Inscription and Symbolic Control.* London: Routledge.

Foucault, M. (1977) *Discipline and Punish: The Birth of the Prison.* London: Allen Lane.

Frowe, I. (2001) 'Language and educational practice', *Cambridge Journal of Education*, 31 (1): 89–102.

Frowe, I. (2001) 'Language and educational research', *Journal of Philosophy of Education Society of Great Britain*, 35 (May):175–90.

Gadamer, H.G. (1979) *Truth and Method.* London: Sheed & Ward.

Gadamer, H.G. (1986) *The Relevance of the Beautiful and Other Essays.* Trans. R. Bernasconi. Cambridge: Cambridge University Press.

Gardner, P.W. (1984) *The Lost Elementary Schools of Victorian Britain: The People's Education.* Beckenham: Croom Helm.

Garrison, J. (1997) *Dewey and Eros: Wisdom and Desire in the Art of Teaching.* New York and London: Teachers College Press.

Gill, S. (1998) *Wordsworth and the Victorians.* Oxford: Clarendon Press.

Gleeson D. and Husbands, C. (2001) *The Performing School: Managing, Teaching and Learning in a Performance Culture.* London: RoutledgeFalmer.

Gomersall, M. (1997) *Working-Class Girls in Nineteenth-Century England: Life, Work and Schooling.* Basingstoke: Macmillan.

Greene, M. (1995) Releasing the Imagination. San Franciso, CA: Jossey-Bass.

Grice, H.P. (1989) *Studies in the Way of Words.* Cambridge, MA: Harvard University Press.

Hadow Report (1931) London: HMSO. Available from www.dg.dial.pipex.com/documents/hadow/31.shtml.

Hargreaves, A. and Fullen, M. (1998) *What's Worth Fighting For in Education?* Buckingham: Open University Press.

Hart, S., Dixon, A., Drummond, M.J. and McIntyre, D. (2004) *Learning Without Limits*. Maidenhead: Open University Press.

Hartley, D. (1749) *Observations on Man, his Frame, his Duty and his Expectations*. Facsimile of 1791 edition in 1998 edition. Poole and Washington, DC: Woodstock Books.

Heaford, M.R. (1967) *Pestalozzi: His Thought and Its Relevance Today*. London: Methuen.

Heidegger, M. (1962) *Being and Time*. Oxford: Basil Blackwell.

Heidegger, M. (1978) 'The origins of the work of art', in F.D. Krell (ed.), *Martin Heidegger Basic Writings*. London: Routledge and Kegan Paul. pp. 160–80.

Her Majesty's Stationery Office (HMSO) (2000) *National Curriculum Handbook for Primary Teachers in England*. London: HMSO.

Hilton, M. (ed.) (1996) *Potent Fictions: Children's Literacy and the Challenge of Popular Culture*. London: Routledge.

Hilton, M. (2007) *Women and the Shaping of the Nation's Young; Education and Public Doctrine in Britain 1750–1850*. Aldershot and Burlington, VT: Ashgate.

Hilton, M. and Hirsch, P. (eds) (2000) *Practical Visionaries: Women, Education and Social Progress 1790–1930*. Harlow: Pearson Education.

Holmes, E. (1911) *What Is and What Might Be*. London: Constable and Co.

Hopkins, D. (2005) *Personalised Learning – How Can We Help Every Child do Even Better*, www.qca.org.uk/11468.html.

Joas, H. (1996) *The Creativity of Action*. Oxford: Blackwell.

Kearney, R. and Rainwater, M. (eds) (1996) *The Continental Philosophy Reader*. London: Routledge.

King, R. (1978) *All Things Bright and Beautiful? A Sociological Study of Infants' Classrooms*. Chichester: John Wiley and Sons.

Kress, G. (1997) *Before Writing: Rethinking the Paths to Literacy*. London: Routledge.

Lawrence, E. (ed.) (1952) *Friedrich Froebel and English Education*. London: Routledge and Kegan Paul.

Liebschner, J. (1991) *The Foundations of Progressive Education*. Cambridge: Lutterworth Press.

Liebschner, J. (1992) *A Child's Work: Freedom and Play in Froebel's Educa-*

tional Theory and Practice. Cambridge: Lutterworth Press.

Locke, J. (1690) *An Essay Concerning Human Understanding*. London.

Locke, J. (1693) *Some Thoughts Concerning Education*. London; edited with introduction and notes by R.H. Quick, Cambridge, 1880.

Lowndes, G.A.N. (1937) *The Silent Social Revolution: An Account of the Expansion of Public Education in England and Wales 1895–1935*. London: Oxford University Press.

Luke, A. (1994) 'Introduction', in A. Freeman and P. Medway (eds), *Genre and the New Rhetoric*. London: Taylor and Francis. pp. i–xi.

Macaulay, C. (1790) *Letters on Education with Observations on Religious and Metaphysical Subjects*. London: C. Dilley.

Macmurray, J. (1935) 'The personal life', *Reason and Emotion*. London: Faber. pp. 93–115.

Macmurray, J. (1961) *Persons in Relation*. London: Faber.

Manton, J. (1976) *Mary Carpenter and the Children of the Streets*. London: Heinemann.

Marcuse, H. (1977) *The Aesthetic Dimension*. Boston, MA: Beacon Press.

Marenz-Bulow, B. (1868) *Child and Child Nature: Contributions to the Understanding of Froebel's Educational Theories* (2nd edn.) Berlin, 1878. Trans. by A. Christie, London, 1879.

McCann, P. (ed.) (1977) *Popular Education and Socialization in the Nineteenth Century*. London: Methuen.

Merleau-Ponty, M. (1996) 'Preface' to 'Phenomenology of perception', in R. Kearney and M. Rainwater (eds), *The Continental Philosophy Reader*. London: Routledge. pp. 79–92.

Miliband, D. (2004) 'Choice and voice in personalised learning'. Speech to the DfES/DEMOS/OECD Conference on Personalising Education: the future of public sector reform, London, 18 May, pp. 3–4.

Miller, J. (1996) *School for Women*. London: Virago.

Morgan, J. (1986) *Godly Learning: Puritan Attitudes towards Reason, Learning and Education, 1560–1640*. Cambridge: Cambridge University Press.

Murray, E.R. (1912) *A Story of Infant Schools and Kindergartens*. London: Sir Isaac Pitman.

National Advisory Committee on Creative and Cultural Education (NACCE) (1999) *All Our Futures: Creativity, Culture and Education*. London: DfEE.

National Campaign for the Arts website at www.artscampaign.org.uk.

Nias, J. (1989) *Primary Teachers Talking: A Study of Teaching as Work*. London: Routledge.

Noddings, N. (1984) *Caring: A Feminine Approach to Ethics and Moral*

Education. Berkeley, CA: University of California Press.

Passmore, J. (1980) *The Philosophy of Teaching*. London: Duckworth.

Passmore, J. (1998) 'Cultivating imagination', in P.H. Hirst and P. White (eds), *Philosophy of Education: Major Themes in the Analytic Tradition*. 4 vols. London: Routledge. Vol. 2, pp. 234–52.

Pestalozzi, J.H. (1900) *How Gertrude Teaches her Children*. Trans. E. Cooke. 2nd edn. London: Swan Sonnerschein.

Peters, R. (ed.) (1969) *Perspectives on Plowden*. London: Routledge and Kegan Paul.

Peters, R.S. (1966) *Ethics and Education*, London: George Allen and Unwin.

Phillips, R. and Furlong, J. (eds) (2001) *Education, Reform and the State: Twenty-five Years of Politics, Policy and Practice*. London: Routledge-Falmer.

Plowden Report (1967) *Children and Their Primary Schools*. London: HMSO. Available at www.dg.dial.pipex.com/documents/plowden.shtml.

Plumb, J.H. (1982) 'The new world of children', in N. McKendrick, J. Brewer and J.H. Plumb, *The Birth of a Consumer Society: The Commercialisation of Eighteenth-Century England*. London: Hutchinson. pp. 286–315.

Pollock, L. (1983) *Forgotten Children: Parent–Child Relations from 1500 to 1900*. Cambridge: Cambridge University Press.

Pullman, P. (2001) *His Dark Materials*. London: Scholastic.

Read, J. (2003) 'Froebelian women: networking to promote professional status and educational change in the nineteenth century', *History of Education*, 32: 17–33.

Reimer, B. (1992) 'What knowledge is of most worth in the Arts?', *The Arts, Education and Aesthetic Knowing*. Edited by B. Reimer and R.A. Smith, editor for the Society, K.J. Rehage. Chicago, IL: NSSE 91st Yearbook.

Retnick J., Cocklin, B. and Coombe K. (eds) (1999) *Learning Communities in Education*. London: Routledge.

Richards, C. (ed.) (2001) *Changing English Primary Education: Retrospect and Prospect*. Stoke-on Trent: Trentham.

Ronge, B. and Ronge, J. (1855) *A Practical Guide to the English Kindergarten: Being an Exposition of Froebel's System*. London: Hodson.

Rousseau, J.-J. (1762) *Emile*. Trans. by B. Foxley. Everyman Edition (1993) London: J.M. Dent.

Schofield, R. (1963) *The Lunar Society of Birmingham: A Social History of*

Provincial Science and Industry in Eighteenth-Century England. Oxford: Clarendon Press.

Scruton, R. (1974) *Art and Imagination: A Study in the Philosophy of Mind*. London: Methuen.

Senge, P., Ronge, B. and Ronge, J., Cambron-McCabe, N., Lucas, T., Smith, B., Dutton, J. and Kleiner, A. (2000) *Schools That Learn*. London: Nicholas Brealey.

Sergiovani, T. (2005) *Strengthening the Heartbeat: Leading and Learning Together in Schools*. San Francisco, CA: Jossey-Bass.

Sharp, R. and Green, G. (1975) *Education and Social Control: A study in Progressive Primary Education*. London: Routledge and Kegan Paul.

Silber, K. (1960) *Pestalozzi: The Man and his Work*. London: Routledge and Kegan Paul.

Silcock, P. (1999) *New Progressivism*. London: Falmer Press.

Silverman, H. (1991) *Gadamer and Hermeneutics*. London: Routledge.

Simon, B. (1960) *Studies in the History of Education 1780–1870*. 2 vols. London: Lawrence and Wishart.

Simon, B. (1991) *Education and the Social Order*. London: Lawrence and Wishart.

Smith, F. (1931) *A History of English Elementary Education 1760–1902*. London: University of London Press.

Steedman, C. (1985) '"The Mother Made Conscious": the historical development of a primary school pedagogy', *History Workshop Journal*, 20: 149–63.

Steedman, C. (1990) *Childhood, Culture and Class in Britain: Margaret McMillan, 1860–1931*. London: Virago.

Sturt, M. (1967) *The Education of the People: A History of Primary Education in England and Wales in the Nineteenth Century*. London: Routledge and Kegan Paul.

Sutherland, G. (1971) *Elementary Education in the Nineteenth Century*. London: Historical Association.

Sutherland, G. (1984) *Ability, Merit and Measurement ... Mental Testing 1880–1940*. Oxford: Oxford University Press.

Taylor, C. (1989) *Sources of Self*. Cambridge: Cambridge University Press.

Taylor, C. (1991) *The Ethics of Authenticity*. Cambridge, MA: Harvard University Press.

Taylor, C. (1992) 'Heidegger, language, and ecology', in H.L. Dreyfus and H. Hall (eds), *Heidegger: A Critical Reader*. Oxford: Blackwell. pp. 247–69.

Tomlinson, S. (2001) *Education in a Post-welfare Society*. Buckingham: Open University Press.

Trouille, M.Seidman. (1997) *Sexual Politics in the Enlightenment: Women Writers Read Rousseau*. Albany, NY: State University of New York Press.

Tymms, P. (2004) 'Are standards rising in English primary schools?', *British Educational Research Journal*, 30: 477–94.

Uglow, J. (2002) *The Lunar Men: The Friends Who Made the Future*. London: Faber and Faber.

Vincent, D. (1989) *Literacy and Popular Culture 1760–1914*. Cambridge: Cambridge University Press.

Walkerdine, V. and Lucey, H. (1989) *Democracy in the Kitchen: Regulating Mothers and Socializing Daughters*. London: Virago.

Warnke, G. (1987) *Gadamer Hermeneutics, Tradition and Reason*. Stanford, CA: Stanford University Press.

Warnock, M. (1994) *Imagination and Time*. Oxford: Blackwell.

Welton, D. (1999) *The Body*. Oxford: Blackwell.

Whitbread, N. (1972) *The Evolution of the Nursery-Infant School*. London: Routledge and Kegan Paul.

White, J. (1992) 'Creativity', in D.E. Cooper (ed.), *A Companion to Aesthetics*. Oxford: Blackwell. pp. 88–91.

White, J. (1993) 'The arts, well-being and education', in R. Barrow and P. White (eds), *Beyond Liberal Education: Essays in Honour of Paul H. Hirst*. London: Routledge. pp. 169–83.

White, J. (2002) *The Child's Mind*. London: RoutledgeFalmer.

Winch, C. and Gingell, J. (1999) *Key Concepts in the Philosophy of Education*. London: Routledge.

Wollons, R. (ed.) (2000) *Kindergartens and Cultures: The Global Diffusion of an Idea*. New Haven, CT, and London: Yale University Press.

Wollstonecraft, M. (1792) *A Vindication of the Rights of Woman*. London: J. Johnson.

Woodham-Smith, P. (1952) 'The origin of the kindergarten', in E. Lawrence (ed.), *Friedrich Froebel and English Education*. London: Routledge and Kegan Paul. pp. 15–34.

Woods, D. and Orlik, S. (1994) *School Review and Inspection*. London: Kogan Page.

Wordsworth, W. (1805) *The Prelude; Book First: Childhood and School-time*. London.

Young, M.F.D. (1998) *The Curriculum of the Future: From the 'New Sociology of Education' to a Critical Theory of Learning*. London: Falmer.

index